D1231715

Nelson's blood

The story of
naval rum
by A J Pack

Naval
Institute
Press

Nelson's blood

**Cover and title page illustrations are from
Rowlandson's 'Nelson feasting with his sailors
after the Battle of the Nile'**

First published in the UK by Kenneth Mason
The old harbourmaster's, Emsworth, Hampshire
© A J Pack 1982, reprinted October 1983
Published and distributed in the United States of America by
the Naval Institute Press, Annapolis, Maryland 21402

Library of Congress Catalog Card No. 82-61669
ISBN 0-87021-944-8

This edition is authorized for sale only in the United States and
its territories and possessions and Canada

Designed by Geoff M Sadler MSIAD
Typeset and produced by Articulate Emsworth
and printed by Southern Publishing Company,
(Westminster Press Ltd), Brighton England

ISBN 0-87021-944-8

Contents

Foreword

The sailor's rum ration, so much a part of the life and image of the Royal Navy for over 300 years, has become a nostalgic memory. In this fascinating and comprehensive book, Captain Pack sets the story of the tot against a background of our maritime history throughout that period — wars, bloody battles, keeping the peace, long voyages of exploration and scientific research — a period that saw the rise of Empire and transition to Commonwealth.

Life at sea was hard and tough; the daily tot not only compensated for the cold and wet, the hard tack and ships biscuit, but also helped to keep Jack's morale high — and it was by the fortitude and strength of such men that the seas were kept free for our seaborne trade. However, as steam replaced sail, social changes ashore and afloat and the increasing sophistication of equipment continually called into question the need for the daily issue of grog. I join those who believe that its abolition was at least twenty years too late.

I was first introduced to the tot as a midshipman during the last war. When the Mediterranean Fleet battleships were in Alexandria, their picket boats would carry out anti-submarine patrols at the seaward end of the Great Pass — the channel leading to the harbour — and, being detached for the statutory twenty four hours, the crews took their rum ration with them. It was clear from the eagerness with which they offered to swop a tot of their rum for a bottle of my gunroom beer that not all sailors considered rum to be the only desirable drink — and I'm glad to say that it is now too late for me to be arraigned for this offence against the regulations!

Many years later, command of an aircraft carrier finally convinced me that rum was an anachronism in the modern navy. The ship and her aircraft were packed with complex systems requiring a clear head and steady hand for both operation and maintenance. A well-drilled flight deck crew demonstrates the highest degree of team training and professional skill demanded from any group of servicemen, and there is no place for slow reactions or bad judgement. Rum was not issued until flying was over for the day and all understood the reason why.

I was at sea again in the Far East Fleet when the fateful decision was announced — no more rum. I have in my scrapbook a photograph of the then First Sea Lord, Admiral Sir Michael Le Fanu, on a visit to the Fleet and surrounded by cheerful sailors with 'Save our Tot' emblazoned on their T-shirts — he didn't take the hint. When the day arrived, my flagship, HMS Blake, like many other ships, gave the tot a fitting farewell with a full ceremonial 'Up Spirits', the participants in a variety of imaginative rigs.

From the start of the new regime, all but the saltiest of old salts among the senior rates appreciate the freedom to have a gin and tonic at mid-day or a whisky and soda in the evening

— or indeed nothing at all — instead of the obligatory 'neaters'; while the junior rates, able to buy up to three cans of beer a day, found this more than ample.

The Sailors' Fund, established by the lump sum compensation for giving up the tot, contributes enormously to the well-being of sailors and their families; swimming pools, sports gear, disco equipment, coach trips in foreign ports, even a golf course, have all been financed from the Tot Fund. This book reveals (to me for the first time) the names of those who so skilfully conducted the negotiations with the Treasury on Jack's behalf. If ever two men deserve a statue erected by grateful sailors they must surely be Admiral Sir Frank Twiss and Sir Michael Carey.

Pusser's Rum isn't dead. Thanks to the imagination and initiative of Charles Tobias; the Admiralty Board who permitted him to use the formula; and not least E D and F Man, the original Admiralty rum broker, old sailors — and modern ones — can still have a nostalgic tot of Nelson's Blood. As they savour the unique flavour and feel the warm glow they can take added satisfaction from the knowledge that the Tot Fund benefits from the royalties.

In today's ships the spirit room is full of beer whilst the tot, like HMS Victory,has become part of naval history. For today's navy that is its rightful place.

Terence Lewin

ADMIRAL OF THE FLEET
Chief of the defence staff

Acknowledgements

I particularly wish to thank Admiral of the Fleet Sir Terence Lewin, the Chief of the Defence Staff, for so generously agreeing to write the Foreword. His high qualification for commenting on any aspect of naval life or history, has been recognised by his appointment as a Trustee of the National Maritime Museum, Greenwich. No less distinguished is the handsome contribution to this book given by Admiral Sir Frank Twiss, who was Second Sea Lord in the days which led to the abolition of naval rum in 1970. His factual, human account provides an authenticity which the author is indeed fortunate to be able to include.

Mr R D Ridding, lately of the Navy's Victualling Department, and a veritable fountain of knowledge on historical aspects of naval diet, has been of immense help not only on the procurement and stowage of rum in the victualling yards, but also in providing the bulk of the information for writing the appendices on Beer and the Cooper's Art.

Likewise Mr Michael Fogg, of E D and F Man, for so long the sole rum brokers to the Admiralty, has given freely of his knowledge, and granted permission for the exclusive use of many stories connected with a special 'Tot Tale Contest' organised by his company.

Overseas friends have made notable contributions, outstandingly so by James Cheevers, the Senior Curator of the US Naval Academy Museum, Annapolis, Luc Marie Bayle, the Director of the Musée de la Marine, Paris, and Commander F C Van Oosten, Director of Naval History to the Royal Netherlands Navy.

On my old familiar stamping ground in Portsmouth, I am

9

indebted to Colin White and Nicola Scadding of the Royal Naval Museum for general help, and to Lieutenant Commander J A Barker, RN, latterly Commanding Officer of Nelson's old flagship, *HMS Victory,* whose acquaintance with the daily rum ritual would suggest that he has enjoyed many a traditional tot in his time.

Gieves and Hawkes have kindly consented to the use of the silhouettes which grace the book's pages, and I am also grateful to the staff of the Naval Historical Library for assistance freely given.

The illustrations have been provided in the main by the Royal Naval Museum, Portsmouth, and the National Maritime Museum, Greenwich but a special acknowledgement is due to Mr John McCarthy for permission to reproduce the picture on page 28, to Lieutenant Commander R Swift RN (Retd) for that of Stan Laurel joining the rum queue, and to the Britannia RN College, Dartmouth for the portrait of Admiral of the Fleet Sir Michael Le Fanu.

Commander Murray Halley, OBE, RN, my close neighbour, has read my typescript with great patience and offered valued criticism. Above all, I owe immense gratitude to my wife for her endless encouragement and help.

A J PACK
Forest Gate, Wickham, Hampshire

10

The boast of Old England,
    the pride of our Queen
The shield of her freedom and glory,
        Her gallant defender — The Navy, I mean
Whose deeds are recorded in story
        Her race on the ocean
        has won every prize
No foe could her strength e'er dissever
        then fill up a bumper
        Britannia, arise!
Here's the Queen and the Navy for ever!

Admiral Sir Edward Vernon, the father
of grog, who started a tradition in the
Royal Navy which lasted two centuries

CHAPTER ONE
Old Grogram
1655 - 1763

A COLD SOUTH-WESTERLY sweeping up the channel caught the fleet head on. Around the flagship another thirty-seven men-of-war struggled into position for their trip across the Atlantic. It was Christmas Day 1654 and Vice-Admiral William Penn's fleet with 3000 soldiers aboard was bound for the sunnier climes of the West Indies.

There were two reasons for the fleet's departure. To many Cromwell's rule in England was so distasteful that he found it necessary to create diversions oversea. What better than an aggressive policy of colonial expansion in the West Indies where Spanish influence was paramount, especially now that the war with the Dutch, the second that century, was over?

Penn's fleet arrived at Barbados, then the most important British base in the West Indies, in late January, 1655 following a remarkably fine and — for those days — trouble-free passage. After embarking more troops, the force proceeded to Hispaniola and landed army units in an attempt to take possession of the Spanish-held island of San Domingo. The ill-prepared attack failed; and a plan for a second attack, which Penn was prepared to undertake, was rejected by the army commander. Reluctant to return to England empty-handed, the admiral decided in May, 1655 to attack Jamaica. Unwilling to leave himself a hostage to fortune, he took the precaution of bombarding the land fortifications before disembarking the army. The softening-up tactics succeeded and after the conquest of the island, which was completed in a month, the main part of the fleet was able to return to England leaving behind a few ships to deal with any Spanish incursion.

The year and the place are important, for it was at Jamaica in 1655 that rum was first issued on board ships of the Royal Navy and, as it happened, quite unofficially.

The reasons for the issue are clear for on leaving home shores, the sailor had recourse only to two forms of liquid refreshment while at sea — water and beer. As with all items which formed part of the daily food ration, these were supplied in wooden casks. The quantities taken on board depended entirely on how much could be stowed conveniently below decks, and were at the captain's discretion. Water could be replenished only when the ship arrived at her destination, or possibly at intermediate ports of call as, at that time, no method of distilling water was known. Furthermore it could not be preserved and rapidly became undrinkable, and the sources from which it was drawn were so varied that often it was foul from the outset. After standing in casks it would quickly putrify, turn slimy and develop algae. No techniques existed for sweetening it and yet, paradoxically, it was usually drunk after the beer stocks ran out.

The ration of beer stood at an ample gallon a day but being of poor quality it was apt to sour within weeks. Moreover, away from home, stocks could rarely be renewed. Thus, there was only one answer: to drink the beer first, because the water, no matter how bad, could be flavoured later with something to make it less offensive — but with beer, never. Small wonder then that in 1588 Lord Howard had written to the Admiralty, 'Nothing doth displease the seamen so as to sour beer.'

Beer was classified either as small beer (because it was weak) or strong beer which kept better and was slightly more expensive. Strong beer was always provided, as one would expect, for ships going overseas, but the contractors who brewed it for the navy were often corrupt and without scruple and the worts for the infusion of malt to ferment the brew into strong beer were appropriated for their own use. Water was added so that the seamen were given in effect small beer, even though they were destined for service abroad and entitled to the stronger variety. Because of expanding maritime trade from about 1650 onwards and the need for overseas bases, the Royal Navy increasingly sent squadrons abroad. However, these ventures lacked compensating amenities to make life more tolerable aboard, and simply added to the misery of the sailor's life afloat.

Rum had one big advantage over beer and water: it remained

sweet for so much longer. When abroad captains of ships were allowed to replace beer with unfortified wine, sometimes, it is believed, even with brandy; but neither was available in the West Indies. Rum, however, was, and thus became the natural alternative to beer for ships serving in this increasingly important part of the world, even though the Victualling Board, thousands of miles away, had not yet sanctioned its use.

Details of rum issues in British warships following the capture of Jamaica in 1655 are obscure and remained so until well into the eighteenth century. This is not really surprising for before 1731 there were no standard regulations or code of instructions for the Royal Navy. Until that time, commanders-in-chief issued their own, so that any rules on the provision of rum, had they existed, would have been of local origin. Additionally the life of a seaman in those days was primitive and was one of hardship. Thus a station such as the West Indies — and particularly the Caribbean with its debilitating climate and high sickness rate — discouraged the retention of a standing force even when there were sufficient ships to provide one. Fleets were sent only if urgent national or political considerations dictated it.

Under Elizabeth I privateering (a form of armed private enterprise afloat) had been tacitly and gratefully accepted by the Queen as an additional source of income but its adoption meant exchanging control for material benefit. The lax discipline frequently found in privateers contrasted with the stricter routine of warships and affected the Navy adversely. Cromwell, as with most autocrats, needed to tighten the rein. An attempt was made to oversee privateering by placing their vessels under naval officers but inevitably this failed. In the West Indies and Caribbean privateers traded in rum and many of these crews turned into buccaneers and pirates. But rum was a seaman's drink as any reader of *Treasure Island* will know, and it was only natural that a fondness for the liquor should have spread rapidly through the navy itself.

Rum derives its name from the Latin *saccharum* meaning sugar, but it was also known in an early form as 'rumbustion' — a seventeenth century word believed to have originated in the sugar cane plantations. After the bulk of the sugar had been extracted from the cane the residue made a 'wash' which was fermented and distilled. During fermentation the spirit developed the characteristic flavour which distinguished it from other liquors, and the longer it was kept the better it became.

One can only guess at the strength of the spirit then issued in those days, but it must have been raw indeed compared with the sophisticated blends issued by the navy of later years. In fact, it was impossible to establish the proof (or strength) of naval rum accurately until 1816, at which time the Sikes' hydrometer was invented. For many years prior to this, the ship's purser or 'pusser' as he was called was responsible for testing and issuing rum at proof by a rough rule of thumb method said to have been invented at the Royal Arsenal. Pure rum was mixed with a little water to which was added a few black gunpowder grains, so that when the sun heated the mixture through a burning glass, the gunpowder just ignited but did no more. Legend has it that in carrying out this test, the explosion of too strong a mixture would blow a purser sky-high allowing everyone to help himself! Too weak a mixture failed to ignite, and the purser could be punished for watering the rum.

From 1600 until the end of the Civil War in England, the navy had been in decline but remarkable support was now given by the Commonwealth government which spent more than half the country's income upon the sea service. At no other period in the navy's long history was this percentage rivalled. Even towards the end of Queen Victoria's reign, which, too, followed a long period of neglect, less than a quarter of the national income was allocated to the navy at a time when other countries were flexing their limbs and spending vast sums in expanding their fleets.

The Commonwealth navy was particularly notable for the sense of professionalism it encouraged among officers and men. It provided promising officers with career opportunities which they had not had before, and it was generous with pay. A shortage of senior officers with experience at sea compelled the use of land officers who were then known as Generals-at-Sea. Fine leaders, of wide attainment, they included Blake who developed into one of Britain's greatest sea captains. It was about this time also that the name 'midshipman' came into being. This title was given to those men with the qualities for promotion from the forecastle to the quarterdeck — midships in this sense, implying half way there. Later the connotation changed with midshipmen denoting an officer's rank, the first rung on the promotion ladder.

Most reforms were instituted as a result of the policy of a new body of Navy Commissioners appointed in 1649. For their day, when corruption was rife, they were remarkably honest. They created a board to look after the sick and wounded where no previous provision had existed, and they were far more generous than their predecessors with rewards, such as prize money. They also reviewed the existing scale of punishments and introduced disciplinary instructions which became known as the Articles of War. Although the code was severe, it was not enforced with the brutality of the later Georgian period when the dreaded 'cat-of-nine-tails' was introduced. Soldiers were frequently embarked for overseas commitments and while at sea they helped work ship. This revealed a need for a standing corps of men who could undertake competently both land and sea service which was met by the formation of the Royal Marines shortly afterwards. Over the years they built for themselves a remarkable reputation for adaptability.

It was to be some time, however, before uniform for officers was introduced, and — almost unbelievably — another two hundred years before the introduction of seamen's uniform. But under the Commonwealth the prices of certain items of standard apparel for seamen (known as slops), were fixed. Contractors not only had to abide by these prices, but also needed a licence from the Navy Commissioners before they could sell them.

A new victualling office was set up and storage buildings were established at the various naval ports, but while much was done to improve victuals through a system of inspection, the quality of both food and drink remained abysmal. Beer was a constant cause for complaint as evidenced by captains' letters of the period which employed the word 'stinking' to emphasise its unwholesomeness.

Life afloat was a living hell when viewed through twentieth-century eyes, but so it was ashore where disease was rife, punishment severe, and starvation round the corner for a great part of the population. The Commonwealth seaman at least developed a self-respect which he had been in danger of losing, a self-respect bolstered by the courage and determination which unquestionably he proved in battle against formidable adversaries — the Dutch.

With the restoration in 1660 of Charles II to a country which had overspent heavily, the navy could no longer expect to receive the favours bestowed by the earlier regime. Failure to honour the pay due to seamen by offering promissory notes, instead of cash, led to a disillusionment which culminated in the ultimate disgrace of the River Medway in 1667, when an unresisted Dutch fleet burned British ships off Chatham, and captured the pride of the Royal Navy, the *Royal Charles* of 100 guns. So profound was the disenchantment among some British seamen that the lure of better and regular pay offered by the Dutch proved too great a temptation. Sadly, the shouts of British voices were not confined to British ships in the Medway melée. Even so, there were later successes at sea which helped rebuild morale so that the outcome of these hard-fought Dutch wars was in Britain's favour and her seaborne trade flourished and expanded as a consequence. In fact, all three wars with Holland had been caused by Britain's enactments of the Navigation Laws which required that produce or manufacture should enter Britain only in the holds of British-built ships manned by British crews. Such acts struck dramatically at the Dutch carrying-trade and were as much an incitement to conflict as they were to be far later with Britain's American cousins.

Although these wars were fiercely fought, the latter half of the seventeenth century was relatively quiescent compared with the one which followed with its never-ending maritime battles. The administration of the navy improved greatly under Samuel Pepys — the shrewd Secretary of the Admiralty who did so much to ease the lot of the seaman and to provide a professional career for officers. In those early days there were no overseas bases of any consequence where ships could be refitted. The only alternative to docking a ship for repair or cleaning was to careen it, but even this operation required a wharf to which the ship could secure if it was to be serviced efficiently. It was, therefore, extremely difficult to maintain a fleet of any size abroad for any length of time.

Jamaica was a case in point. Following its capture in 1655, its potential as a base developed slowly. In 1727, *HMS Greyhound* was at Port Royal where her crew was helping to build a new careening wharf. Local labour was lethargic, and progress was desperately slow as one would expect in a hot, enervating climate. To encourage the sailors to work, Captain Gascoigne of the *Greyhound* wrote to the Navy Board on February 14, 'If anything can make it agreeable to them, it may be a double allowance of rum being joined to what extra pay may be thought proper to give them.' If the ship's company was already receiving half a pint of rum per man per day as an alternative to beer, then Captain Gascoigne was recommending that his men should have a pint of rum each day — to work harder!

A few years later, in 1731, came evidence that when rum was issued as an alternative to the customary beer, the daily allowance was, indeed, half a pint. The Regulations and Instructions Relating to His Majesty's Service at Sea, embodying for the first time standard rules for the navy, contained this reference, 'Of the Provisions. In case it should be thought for the Service to alter any of the foregoing particulars of provisions in ships employed on foreign voyages, it is to be observed that a pint of wine or half a pint of brandy, rum or arrack, hold provision to a gallon of beer.'

The issue of rum on the West Indies station had come to stay, but at this time there is no supporting evidence to show that it was issued more widely.

Well before 1700 it was an axiom that any European power with an interest in the North American littoral needed advance bases in the West Indies. Spain obviously had a head start with its stranglehold in the Caribbean which caused her rivals to cast acquisitive eyes in that direction. Another attraction was the developing trade in commodities which were sources of potential wealth for entrepreneurs of diverse backgrounds, not least the transport of negro slaves from Africa. The French, British, and Dutch, all had island bases. Their successful exploitation and expansion depended on the degree of maritime support which could be given, with military control as the ultimate weapon. National aspirations were one thing, but there was also the problem of appalling piracy which raged out of hand. The best that can be said of Kidd, Thatch (or Blackbeard as he was more commonly called), and other egregious people of that ilk, is that they were fine seamen. The unforgiveable was that legitimate merchants of all nations were their prey and they were, therefore, a pestilence to be eliminated.

After 1655 the British had two island bases in Jamaica and Barbados which offered a reasonable degree of logistic support for visiting warships. The design of ships aimed at improving their sea-keeping and offensive potential had made progress although that splendid maid of all work — the frigate — had still to wait until the middle of the century before making her debut. The number of ships kept on station slowly increased, thereby ensuring a presence and watchful eye but, in emergency or campaign, only a fleet from home could suffice. A certain Captain Edward Vernon, who was to play a vital part in the story of rum, served in the West Indies between 1708 and 1712, commanding the *Jersey* (60 guns).

The overwhelming problem for visiting squadrons was their inability to prevent sickness. Ships, unventilated between decks, were unhealthy in themselves; ideas of sanitation and cleanliness were crude, sometimes non-existent; food consisting mainly of salted meat and infested biscuits was monotonous and liquids well nigh undrinkable. Add to this a debilitating foreign climate with a variety of unpleasant fevers, and it is easy to understand why sickness was the main enemy.

No better illustration could make the point than Vice-Admiral Hosier's expedition in 1726 to the West Indies with a squadron of ships during the time when relations with Spain were severely strained. After a long passage, Hosier's force arrived off Porto Bello where a game of bluff and counter bluff ensued over the sailing of a Spanish treasure fleet. A futile six-month blockade by the British ships was followed by an equally lack-lustre campaign in 1727, which took the most appalling toll of human lives including Admiral Hosier's own. More than 4000 seamen succumbed to fever compared with the handful who died from enemy action. Incredibly, Hosier's body was interred in the ballast of his flagship! Sadly, ignorance of this elementary rule of hygiene caused the fever to spread even further.

Britain's trading interests in the West Indies throughout the 1730's received many setbacks at the hands of the Spanish. On the 'first come' principle, Spaniards had every right to resent the increasing presence of a foreign power with acquisitive designs, but their treatment of those who offended was brutal. Public indignation in England reached a peak in the case of 'Jenkins' Ear'. Richard Jenkins, the master of a merchant brig, the *Rebecca*, claimed on his return that his ear had been cut off by the crew of a Spanish coastguard and that he had been told to take it back to his master the King. Whether or not this was true, the incident was enough to turn strained relations into war, which Britain declared on Spain in 1739.

No time was wasted in mounting a naval expedition to the West Indies under the command of the same Edward Vernon, now a Vice-Admiral. Vernon was a bewildering mixture of out-standing and indifferent qualities. Well-educated, with an impeccable background, he provided a good example of the new type of professional emerging in the senior ranks. He was devoted to the navy but, unable to suffer fools gladly, was also the bane of the establishment. If irritated by the Admiralty he had the habit of criticising Their Lordships in strong language, and he made the fatal mistake of pursuing too openly his political affiliations.

He was adored by the seamen for his humanity and obvious concern for them — a Nelson in miniature. Ahead of his day in the reforms he wished to see carried out, he wrote to the Secre-tary of the Admiralty on impressment in particular, begging a more humane system of recruiting. In return for his concern for the welfare of those under him, he expected high standards — and got them.

He was a good tactician and interpreter of the Fighting Instructions, and gained an instant success at Porto Bello primarily through his ability to give clear written instructions to his captains about his intentions. Porto Bello, the main entrepôt for Spanish trade, was selected for attack because Vernon learned that a large assignment of gold and silver had been sent there from Panama. The remarkable sequel, which followed the town's capture, was Vernon's decision that all public money found was to be divided fairly as prize among those British crews which took part in the engagement. This was a brave step, in defiance of the regulations, but general delight at home over the victory caused it to be overlooked. No act could have done more to win the sailors' hearts. Vernon behaved with equal compas-sion towards the inhabitants of Porto Bello: no looting was allowed and everyone — including the military and clergy — was protected from abuse.

The Porto Bello success was timely and caused a modest euphoria in England much the same as that later and greater event at Trafalgar. Both raised sagging morale and Vernon gained much kudos from his victory. Yet it is for a much more mundane reason that his name lingers on — his link with the naval rum ration.

By 1740 the rum issue, as the daily alternative to beer, was common practice on the West Indies station. Seamen drank the raw spirit in drams, one gulp with no heel-taps, a practice inconsistent with shipboard work and sobriety and the cause of many accidents in the rigging when ships were at sea. In port the troubles were even greater. Shore leave was prohibited, not that authority was inhumane, but simply that most pressed men would never return if given the opportunity. As a quid pro quo ladies were allowed on board for the night. In one instance it is recorded that the captain of a frigate sent ashore for 300 black women to sup and sleep in his ship. Lack of shore leave brought with it an attendant vice — smuggling. In Jamaica, for example, rum was cheap and plentiful and a little ingenuity ensured its undiscovered arrival aboard. One simple ruse which was easily executed with the aid of a drill, was to remove the milk from coconuts and refill them with rum. Clearly Vernon had a problem on his hands and he was not slow in grasping the nettle. Before taking any action he wisely consulted his captains and surgeons on the step he proposed. His solution was to end the drinking of rum in drams by enforcing its mixture with water before issue. Once he had obtained everyone's agreement, a General Order was issued,

'349. Order to Captains
(Copy from Public Records Office. Adm./I/232)

Burford, at Port Royal,
August 21, 1740

Whereas it manifestly appears by the returns made to my general order of the 4th of August, to be the unanimous opinion of both Captains and Surgeons, that the pernicious custom of the seamen drinking their allowance of rum in drams, and often at once, is attended with many fatal effects to their morals as well as their health, which are visibly impaired thereby, and many of their lives shortened by it, besides the ill consequences arising from stupefying their rational qualities, which makes them heedlessly slaves to every passion; and which have their unanimous opinion cannot be better remedied than by ordering their half pint of rum to be daily mixed with a quart of water, which they that are good husbandmen, may, from the saving of their salt provisions and bread, purchase sugar and limes to make more palatable to them.

'You are therefore hereby required and directed, as you tender both the spiritual and temporal welfare of his Majesty's subjects, and preserving sobriety and good discipline in his Majesty's

Service, to take particular care that rum be no more served in specie to any of the ship's company under your command, but that the respective daily allowance of half a pint a man for all your officers and ship's company, be every day mixed with the proportion of a quart of water to every half pint of rum, to be mixed in a scuttled butt kept for that purpose, and to be done upon deck, and in the presence of the Lieutenant of the Watch, who is to take particular care to see that the men are not defrauded in having their full allowance of rum, and when so mixed it is to be served to them in two servings in the day, the one between the hours of 10 and 12 in the morning, and the other between 4 and 6 in the afternoon.

'And you are to take care to have other scuttled butts to air and sweeten their water for their drinking at other times, and to give strict charge to your Lieutenants in their respective Watches to be very careful to prevent any rum and all spirituous liquors being privately conveyed on board the ship by your own boats or any others, and both you and they must expect to answer for the ill-consequences that may result from any negligence in the due execution of these orders. Given etc.

EV'

There are some interesting points in this order beyond its

Women aboard a man-of-war watch sailors milling between decks. No shore leave given!

main purpose. First, was the encouragement to add sugar and limes to the mixture to make it more palatable. Could it be that, as early as 1740, the antiscorbutic property of limes was already receiving some official recognition? If so, it would seem that Vernon belonged to the converted. Second, was the warning that men were not to be defrauded of their rum allowance. This served notice that the spirit, even mixed with water, was part of the daily ration and thus sacrosanct. For opportunists, perhaps particularly the purser, 'beware!' was surely the message of his order. Third, was the requirement to have scuttled butts (the forerunner of the tub), to air and sweeten the water normally kept in cask below, for the seamen to drink at other times. Could this have been an enlightened innovation of Vernon's? It would have been in line with his progressive thinking on such matters. Lastly, came the warning to prevent the smuggling of liquor onboard; that failure to enforce this order would have drastic consequences for any officer or man caught. Vernon was serving notice that consumption of rum in drams was not the only problem, and that officers, too, were not beyond the law when it came to smuggling.

At first the new system was unpopular, for the sailor has always had a conservative attitude towards change in food and drink. But accepted it was and the average man must have benefited. Although drunkenness did not disappear it certainly became less prevalent. Added to this, watered rum helped marginally to reduce the sickness rate which was also Vernon's aim.

The mixture had to have a name and, with the seaman's traditional flair for invention, one was swiftly coined. Vernon's own nickname Old Grogram, on account of the waterproof boat-cloak he wore, provided 'grog' which entered the sailor's vocabulary. If the Oxford dictionary definition of grogram is to be believed — 'coarse fabric of silk, mohair and wool, or these mixed, often stiffened with gum' — then poor Vernon must have sweated under the West Indian sun.

Admiral Vernon fell out of favour towards the end of his career when his tactlessness in dealing with higher authority increased but he deserves to be remembered for his virtues — his love for the British seaman and his perspicacity in realising what was good for the navy. Desertion was ever a problem — as it was bound to be among men unwillingly pressed into service. It was most

24

A painting of Admiral Edward Vernon by Charles Philips who specialised in portraits of the aristocracy and politicians. Vernon, himself, was a Member of Parliament for some time

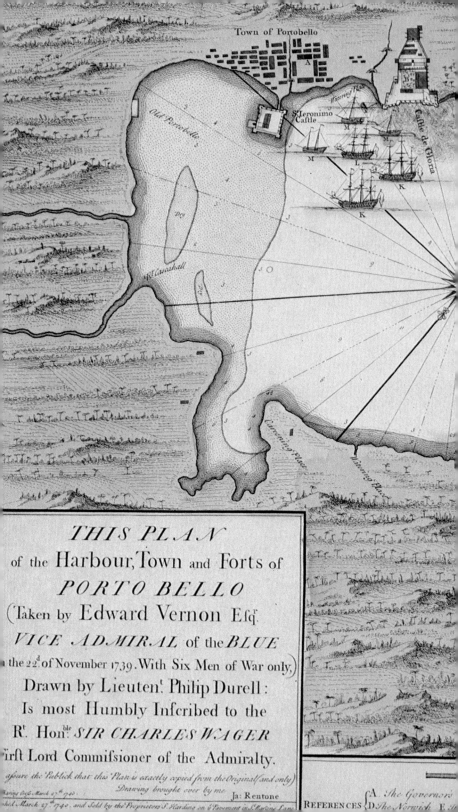

Town of Portobello

St Heronimo Castle

Castle de Gloria

Old Portobello

THIS PLAN
of the Harbour, Town and Forts of
PORTO BELLO
(Taken by Edward Vernon Esq.
VICE ADMIRAL of the *BLUE*
a the 22.ᵈ of November 1739. With Six Men of War only)
Drawn by Lieuten.ᵗ Philip Durell:
Is most Humbly Inscribed to the
R.ᵗ Hon.ᵇˡᵉ *SIR CHARLES WAGER*
First Lord Commissioner of the Admiralty.

assure the Publick that this Plan is exactly copied from the Originall (and only)
Drawing brought over by me
Ja: Rentone

REFERENCES
A The Governor...
D The Norwich...

Iron Castle

Drakes I.t

F. Durell delin. November 1739.

A Scale of Two English Miles

...s Shot through by one of the lower tier of Guns from the Admirals Ship ỳ Burford B Plantation in ỳ Castle &...
...nodore Browns Ship ỳ Hampton Court G The Strafford H The Princess Louisa I The Sendon K Two Spanish Guarda...

HMS Victory in St Helen's Roads off the Isle of Wight after her return from Trafalgar. The ensign at half-mast indicates that Lord Nelson's body is still on board. Painting by J W Carmichael

(Overleaf) Plan of the harbour and town at Porto Bello, 1739, after a drawing by Lieutenant Philip Durell, RN

prevalent in the West Indies where masters of merchant ships offered substantial bribes to seamen to sail their undermanned vessels home. Vernon observed in a letter to the Admiralty in 1742, '. . . the great reduction of our seamen by death and desertion, not less than 500 having deserted from the hospital in Port Royal since my being in command; which I believe to have all been seduced out and gone home with the homeward bound trade, through the temptations of high wages and 30 gallons of rum, and being generally conveyed drunk onboard their ships from the punch houses where they are seduced.'

Vernon was ever the enemy of 'that formidable Dragon, Drunkenness' as he called it in his letter to Their Lordships, but the extract is also interesting in showing that the locals had learned a thing or two from His Majesty's Impressment Service at home in how to seize their victims!

In 1745 Britain was at war with France and smugglers were particularly active in the towns of Deal, Dover, Ramsgate and Folkestone. Vernon was in command of The Downs, an important but unexciting land-based appointment in East Kent, which Nelson, too, had to suffer at a later period. He wrote with some passion on the subject of smuggling, '. . . this smuggling has converted those employed in it, first from honest, industrious fishermen to lazy, drunken, and profligate smugglers, and now to dangerous spies on all our proceedings, for the enemy's daily information.' And again later, 'there are lawyers who say . . . such an intercourse with His Majesty's enemies is now by our laws high treason; and if so, I should think we want a speedy proclamation to inform these infamous wretches that it is high treason; and they shall be prosecuted as such; for surely, no nation but this would suffer itself to be daily betrayed with impunity.'

In 1756 additional regulations were made to the original 1731 version of The Regulations and Instructions Relating to His Majesty's Service at Sea. As already explained, grog came in with Vernon in 1740, but the 1756 regulations contained the first official ruling from the Admiralty that rum was to be mixed with water. It can be argued, therefore, that grog's official birth occurred in 1756, although Their Lordships required time before they came round to calling it by its new name!

The new rules must have been badly needed, for by 1756 the navy had many more ships serving in North American and West

Indian waters. Ships returning home, or diverted off station, would be carrying full casks of rum, and thus it was that the grog-drinking habit started to spread beyond the West Indies. The new regulations support this theory with orders for the provision of a separate storeroom for the stowage of rum. It had been the custom to stow rum casks on the shingle ballast in the hold, less than satisfactory in wooden ships where fire was ever an enemy. More sensible stowing precautions were necessary along the lines of those for gunpowder where hanging magazines of special construction reduced the likelihood of explosion. Strong spirit has always been a volatile commodity and rum was no exception. It has even been known for cars to use it during times of petrol shortage in the West Indies!

These new regulations for the provision of a spirit room are printed here complete as they make an interesting comparison with those for twentieth-century warships explained in a later chapter.

'The keeping as well as the issuing the said liquors being liable to dangerous accidents, if proper care be not taken; for prevention therefore of such accidents, the storerooms for holding the said liquors, are to be fitted in the following manner, when there is time, opportunity and room to do it; and the other methods hereafter mentioned are to be observed in issuing or starting the said liquors, to wit; the foremost bulkhead of the Fish Room to be removed two or three feet aft, and a bulkhead put up afore it, about five or six feet distance, athwart the Hold, up to the Orlop, to have sufficient rabbit at the ends and sides, with proper bars and locks to secure them; the platform or Orlop over them, and the bulkheads and hatches, to be lined and plaistered in the same manner as those for the Powder Rooms; and the seams of the foot-wailing to be batton'd; and a small store-room lanthorn to be fixed a little below the platform, near the midship part, either in the foremost or aftermost bulkhead, with a small scuttle through the platform, clear of the bulkhead, and an inclosed convenience under the platform, to secure room to put the candle into the lanthorn, at such time as the hatchways

The Sailor's Farewell by Mosley, 1744. Such prints of the eighteenth century were popular with the public

The Sailor's Return, again by Mosley
and complementary to the Farewell
overleaf

do not afford sufficient light to see to sling the casks; which, when the said liquors are wanted, either to be issued to the Ship's Company, or started into smaller cask, are to be hoisted on the upper deck; and whilst that is doing, proper Centinels are to be placed to prevent candles being brought near the hatches while they are open, or near the liquor while it is serving or starting, on the deck; neither of which is ever to be done but by daylight: all Commanders of His Majesty's Ships and Vessels are hereby strictly required and directed to be very careful, that the whole of the said methods be put in execution, if the storerooms can be fitted in the manner aforementioned; but if they cannot be so fitted, all the other precautions, of placing proper Centinels, not suffering candles to be carried near the liquor, causing it always to be issued and started upon the open deck, and never suffering either to be done but by daylight, are to be most punctually observed.'

If Vernon's encouragement to mix lime juice with the grog issue stemmed from a belief that it would help to combat scurvy, then he was a man of remarkable prescience. This pestilential disease had always been prevalent afloat but in the Georgian navy it grew out of hand. The flourishing East India Company was not afflicted so badly as the Royal Navy, despite the long voyages of its ships, thanks to better diet and less overcrowding. Even Drake in his circumnavigation of the world in the tiny *Golden Hind* nearly two centuries before, remained reasonably free from the scourge. In his account, *The World Encompassed*, it is evident that he made the best use of greenstuffs — wild lettuce — when, for example, Drake showed a wisdom the Commissioners of Victualling seemed unable to emulate. On Anson's voyage round the world in the *Centurion* from 1740 to 1743, more than half of the 1955 men who set out from Portsmouth in his squadron were lost, all, it is believed, from scurvy. The disease rendered unfit for duty three times as many as it killed; and an appreciation of how to combat it was slow in coming. The reluctance of the Admiralty to make changes in the daily food ration when all evidence pointed to scurvy being a dietary

33

disease simply exacerbated matters.

The answer was found in 1747 by experiment; which particular diet kept who alive? Success followed a diet of oranges and lemons, but the Admiralty took many more years to learn that lesson and the significance of Vitamin C was not appreciated until more than a century later. In their Additional Regulations of 1756, Their Lordships specified, 'Elixir of Vitriol having been recommended by the College of Physicians as an efficacious medicine in scorbutick cases, and the same being made a part of the invoice of the Surgeon's Sea Chest; the Captain is to order the Surgeon to observe such printed instructions as will be given to them by the Commissioners of the Sick and Hurt, for their guidance in the practice and care of it.'

To the layman vitriol sounds far removed from a remedy — but Their Lordships' recommendation of its use in 1756 was unpardonable when, nine years earlier, experiments had proved its total lack of life-preserving qualities.

In a sense, rum was now of age. Firmly established in the navy as a popular alternative to beer, it had its uses even to the surgeon in sedating his victims prior to amputation! There was an increasing demand for it, although belief in its power as an antidote to scurvy was waning rapidly. Greater control in its issue was now in force, and Vernon's grog had come to stay. Even so, the serving of so large and potent a mixture twice a day presented problems which were to remain unsolved until well into the nineteenth century.

Come cheer up my lads!
    'tis to glory we steer
To add something more
    to this wonderful year
To honour we call you,
    not press you like slaves
For who are so free
    as the sons of the waves?

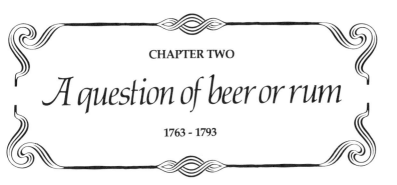

CHAPTER TWO

A question of beer or rum

THE WORDS OVERLEAF by David Garrick from *Hearts Oak* were written to commemorate 1759, the year of victories, the *annus mirabilis* with the Royal Navy's outstanding successes at Quiberon Bay, Quebec and Lagos. Initially the Seven Years' War, starting in 1756, had gone badly for Britain but ended gloriously despite the over-generous peace terms.

Garrick's sentiments are at odds with those of his contemporary Samuel Johnson who, about the same time, was writing, 'No man will be a sailor who has contrivance enough to get himself into jail; for being in a ship is being in jail with the chance of being drowned. A man in jail has more room, better food, and commonly better company.' The contradiction to Garrick's 'who are so free as the sons of the waves?' is as complete as it could be.

The true situation probably lay somewhere between. By present day standards life afloat was certainly crude and bestial but not intolerable, and there had been significant progress since Vernon's day, in which rum had played its part.

One noticeable feature was the emergence of an improved relationship between officers and men. Good leadership has always reaped its rewards, and men such as Hawke and Boscawen, the victors at Quiberon Bay and Lagos, were outstanding leaders and well-trusted by their crews. Firm disciplinarians, they were intelligent men who enforced a better standard of hygiene between decks and supported a greater variety in the seamen's diet. They set an example for those who aspired to become admirals, and from this time until the end of the Napoleonic Wars, Britain was fortunate to possess many of exceptional calibre. The list is long but Rodney, Howe, Hood, St Vincent and Nelson were outstanding, not only in battle but also for the reforms they helped introduce.

A hundred years before, Samuel Pepys had shrewdly observed that, 'Englishmen, and more especially seamen, love their bellies above everything else, and therefore it must always be remembered in the management of the victualling of the navy that to make any abatement from them in the quantity or agreeableness of the victuals is to discourage and provoke them in the tenderest point and will soon render them disgusted with the King's service than any other hardship that can be put upon them.' The victualling commissioners, the contractors they employed, and the shipborne pursers all resisted improvement in the standard ration because the system did not encourage it. Their tenderest point — unlike the seaman — was their pocket and their own profit provided the motive.

A policy of no change in the conditions of service was encouraged further by the fact that seamen were in demand only for wartime service. The lack of a standing navy of long-serving men meant that reform was not considered urgently in peacetime. Consider the following fluctuations in numbers of men in service between 1754 and 1810.

1754 (peace)	10,000
1756 (beginning of war)	53,000
1762 (end of war)	85,000
1764 (peace)	17,000
1775 (peace)	15,000
1783 (war)	107,000
1786 (peace)	13,000
1793 (beginning of war)	70,000
1802 (end of war)	130,000
1803 (temporary peace)	50,000
1810 (war)	142,000

Such a stop-go policy of manning the fleet with pressed men was not conducive to improved living standards. Yet the same period was one of almost unremitting war — each succeeding war demanding more and more men. Probably for this reason, more than any other, improvements in welfare became increasingly necessary.

Until 1756, surgery and medicine in the navy had been rudimentary. During the seven years of war that followed, for every man killed in action, at least eighty were lost by disease or desertion! Scurvy remained the scourge of the navy, and the need for its control became more pressing as the century progressed. The basic internal design of wooden warships had scarcely changed in the 1700's so that even though concepts of hygiene had advanced, it remained difficult to apply them in such out-dated conditions.

Somehow naval surgeons had to face up to the appalling wastage of lives caused through disease. In the latter half of the century their diagnostic achievements were outstanding. Unfortunately, the Admiralty did not respond to their recommendations for improvements with the alacrity the situation deserved, so that it was not until remedies had been proven many times over that they were effected. Much of course rested in the hands of the senior sea officers of the day, so that one would find enlightened captains acting on the advice of their surgeons with resultant benefits to their ships' companies. The reverse was also true and it was commonplace to find extraordinary fluctuations between ships in their sickness rate. Three surgeons stand out for their work and wisdom during this period. James Lind, who became the surgeon in charge of the splendid new Naval Hospital built at Haslar, near Portsmouth, was well ahead of his contemporaries in treatment of scurvy. It was he who also recommended that seamen should wear uniform clothing, not only for appearance's sake but primarily as an aid to cleanliness; although it was to be another 100 years before Lind's proposal was adopted.

Dr Thomas Trotter was another surgeon who carried on the good work of his predecessors and was particularly successful in introducing dietary reforms when serving as Physician of the Channel Fleet at the start of the Revolutionary War, thirty years after Lind. He concentrated on combatting drunkenness which by then had become the principal vice of the British seaman — ashore and afloat. Trotter was no friend of grog and observed that 'it exhausts and debilitates the constitution', particularly of younger seamen. Many seamen had reverted to drinking their spirit in drams whenever possible, contrary to Vernon's diktat of fifty years earlier. But it must also be remembered that any seaman serving in the Channel Fleet at this time would still have been receiving his official ration of beer while afloat and grog only infrequently, so that Trotter's strictures probably tended to apply more to the inferior spirit obtained ashore when ships were in port.

The third naval surgeon to bring about significant reform was Sir Gilbert Blane who, as a younger man, had been Admiral Rodney's personal physician. When Blane was later to become the Commissioner for the Sick and Wounded, he was instrumental, along with Trotter, in persuading the Admiralty to order lemon juice to be issued to all crews proceeding abroad — and not only to the sick as had been the practice before. It sounds a simple enough remedy but it saved countless lives at sea and would have saved more had the evidence of earlier years been acted upon sooner. Wise commanders were quick to take advantage of the new rule, and it is on record that Nelson ordered no less than 50,000 gallons of lemon juice from Sicily for his Mediterranean fleet. It certainly must have been an important factor in making his ships the healthiest afloat at this time.

The recommendation to issue lemon juice duly appeared in the Regulations and Instructions Relating to His Majesty's Service at Sea, 'Lemon Juice at half an ounce per day with sugar at same amount to be allowed when on, or proceeding to, foreign stations and to be mixed with grog or wine — BUT not while beer is being issued.'

This was further confirmation that beer was part of the official ration while grog was not. Once the beer was expended, grog or wine could be issued in lieu, particularly on foreign stations. The West Indies station was no longer alone in the league for grog which had developed almost a mantle of anti-scorbutic respectability through its association with lemon and lime juice.

Despite his success with lemon juice, Blane was also an advocate of beer and wine. Less vehement than Trotter in condemning distilled spirit, he considered it beneficial in cold climates and even commended wine on the West Indies and North America stations as a permanent replacement for rum. Could this have been the thin end of the pledge for dispensing with rum altogether? There is striking confirmation of this from Blane's mentor of earlier days in a letter from Admiral Rodney to Admiralty written from the island of St Eustatius in the West Indies on April 27, 1781, 'The season at present is sickly, and very fatal to the troops lately come from England. Was it possible to supply the ships with wine in this climate thousands of lives might be saved, and the rum would be useful to the seamen in our moist and cold Channel.' One cannot escape the conclusion that Rodney and Blane must have discussed the problem frequently.

The fact is that the rum issue had become firmly established. Furthermore the Admiralty had no problem procuring it and it was cheap. Moreover, seamen now claimed it as their right whenever it was obtainable and it would have been folly for Their Lordships to have interfered with what had now become an accepted custom. In the words of Richard Dana, the nineteenth century American sailor writer, 'Sailors will never be convinced that rum is a dangerous thing, by taking it away from them and giving it to the officers; nor that temperance is their friend, which takes from them what they have always had, and gives them nothing in place of it.'

Blane's knowledge of rum was anything but superficial, 'It is with reason that the new rum is accused of being more unwholesome than what is old; for being long kept, it not only becomes weaker and more mellow by part of the spirit exhaling, but time is allowed for the evaporation of a certain nauseous empyrematic principle (element) which comes over in the distillation, and which is very offensive to the stomach; therefore, though this is the produce of the West India Islands, yet what is supplied there is inferior to that which is brought from England.'

Blane was right of course, for the aging of rum along with its blending became increasingly important in providing a liquor which was acceptable aboard ship until that time when naval rum acquired its vintage quality. The rum broker, the victualling department and the consumer (the seamen themselves), all helped to make it a subject for connoisseurs.

Lind, Trotter and Blane were not the only contributors to the defeat of scurvy and the resultant improvement in the navy's health. There were other ship's surgeons urging similar remedies. Mr William Northcote, surgeon aboard *HMS Prudent* at Sandy Hook, New York, was another. On August 19, 1781 he wrote, 'My Lord — I should not presume to address your lordship (The Earl of Sandwich, First Lord of the Admiralty), was I not persuaded that whatever contributes to promote the health and happiness of so valuable a life as that of a British sailor cannot fail of meeting your lordship's most gracious acceptance, which I flatter myself will in some measure apologize for the liberty I have taken, and that the justness of my intentions will excuse the freedom.

As the Scurvy, my lord, is the most prevalent and most destructive disease incident to seamen, and lemon and orange juice the grand specific in that most terrible malady, I humbly beg leave to recommend it to your lordship's consideration whether it would not be of infinite more service to the navy, if the surgeons of His Majesty's ships were to be largely supplied with those most salutary vegetable acids instead of the present mineral acid (elixir of vitriol), which is of little or no use.

Two thirds of our seamen die of the scurvy. . . .'

As explained previously, experiments carried out in 1747 had shown elixir of vitriol to be no panacea for scurvy but the 1756 Sea Regulations failed to withdraw it and Their Lordships thirty-four years later were still issuing it as an anti-scorbutic.

As rum had come to stay, the question arose of how it was to be obtained and supplied to ships? Ever-widening commitments in the succession of maritime wars required more ships and thus more men. France was sufficiently close to demand the maintenance of a strong British fleet in home waters for both offensive and defensive roles. Blockade of the Brittany coast compelled ships to be kept on station there despite the sometimes appalling weather, a task that was both monotonous and mostly unrewarding. Threats of invasion also required ships to be at readiness in the English Channel and western approaches. Nevertheless, in contrast to the century before, it was overseas that the greatest expansion of maritime activity was taking place. And long before the end of the Napoleonic wars, British warships operated in all five oceans.

The number of ships in naval service, but not necessarily in commission, compare interestingly with the manpower totals given on page 38.

1754 (peace)	296
1756 (beginning of war)	320
1762 (end of war)	432
1775 (peace)	340
1778 (beginning of war)	450
1783 (end of war)	617
1793 (beginning of war)	411
1802 (end of war)	781

| 1803 (temporary peace) | 663 |
| 1810 (war) | 1048 |

Expansions of this kind of course must have caused the demands for rum to increase dramatically.

In the early days of the rum issue — when only ships in West Indian waters qualified — it was supplied directly by the local contractor, and each ship's purser would have had to accept what he was given whatever the price or quality. Some time later when rum had to be supplied on a regular basis in England to ships going abroad, the victualling commissioners, through contractors, organised ship requirements to be sent to dockyards and bases. As they did not handle the rum themselves, however, it was still possible for a ship's purser to be at the mercy of a dishonest contractor. The victualling board had expanded in parallel with the navy until gradually they coalesced, and from 1742 onwards, with its piecemeal move down river from rickety warehouses at Tower Hill to new stores in Deptford, the board was able, if slowly, to extend its direct control of ship supplies. The board was greatly helped by the practice of allowing government stores to be obtained free of duty for ships going overseas, whereby the commissioners could have absolute control of rum supplies. General rules on procedure for receiving and storing spirits duty free were issued by the Treasury in 1782 and all that remained for the victualling board then was to nominate its sole broker for supplying rum under contract. In all probability such an arrangement caused an improvement in the quality of rum, as no broker would have wished to lose such a highly-prized contract.

Yet these developments were not the end of the story. In 1832 far reaching reforms gave The Admiralty more direct control over the civil departments, of which victualling was one. Henceforth the commissioners, no longer autonomous, were responsible instead to a Sea Lord under the new title of Controller of Victualling. As a result of this change, the quality control of everything supplied for the seaman's inner needs became the direct concern of the new controller. It was now for him — and no-one else — to ensure that the taste, colour, and other qualities of rum, gave the seaman what he sought.

During the late eighteenth century, and indeed well into the next, the regulations did not stipulate the quantity of water to be

An 18th century view of the naval yard at Deptford which became the spiritual home of rum!

added to neat rum to make it into grog. 'The due proportion' or 'the usual proportion' were the vague expressions used.

So what was the 'usual proportion'? Although Vernon had ordered a quart of water to half a pint of rum (four to one), later it seems to have become the practice to issue it in the proportion of three to one, although this varied from ship to ship. An extract from the memoirs of Admiral Dillon as a midshipman in *HMS Defence* in 1794, provides a clue, '. . . So soon as the ship was in

order, the grog was served out; but with us the seamen had four portions of water to the spirits whereas three parts was the established custom of the navy. Our captain by altering the allowance as mentioned, was anxious to prevent drunkenness. This did not succeed but only created discontent.'

An extract from *Tars of Old England* by a sailor, Jack Nastyface, relating the routine in *HMS Revenge* at the turn of the century supports the three-to-one theory, 'After punishment, the bos'n's mate pipes to dinner, it being eight bells or twelve o'clock; and this is the pleasantest part of the day, as at one bell the piper is called to play *Nancy Dawson* or some other lively tune, a well known signal that the grog is ready to be served out. It is the duty of the cook from each mess to fetch and serve it out to his messmates of which every man and boy is allowed a pint, that is, one gill of rum and three of water, to which is added lemon acid sweetened with sugar.' The evening ration, of course, was the same, but was served without lemon juice or sugar.

If four-to-one grog resulted in discontent, it is surprising that the custom of issuing it at five-to-one adopted later by Admiral Lord Keith, did not provoke outright mutiny! He, like Vernon, abhorred drunkenness.

The crux of the matter was that when Their Lordships referred to 'the usual proportion of water', they were leaving the decision to individual captains. Three-to-one became customary for years to come, and nearly a century was to pass before the Admiralty prescribed the mixture by regulation. But there was always a tendency to serve even weaker grog. Seamen of course disliked over-watered grog — who would not? — thus it was natural to find that stoppage of grog and the watering of grog continued as a punishment for an exceedingly long time. The following passage provides an old and unique definition for mixing grog,

' "Vy" at length reluctantly said Tom Bennett, "I might be a little hazy last night, but I worn't drunk, I know. How could I be? I had only two north-westers", meaning two glasses of grog, half water, half spirits, 'and a glass due north', meaning all spirits; for the seamen onboard a ship mix their grog by the compass points. For instance due north is raw spirit, due west is water alone; thus although they may ask for more northing, they are rarely known to cry for more westing in their spirited course. WNW consequently is one third spirits and two thirds water; NW half and half; NNW two thirds spirit; and then comes the summum bonum, due north, or spirit alone "neat" '.

The American War of Independence which followed the Seven Years war after fifteen years of peace was a depressing period in the annals of British maritime history. Peacetime had brought little in the way of much-needed reform to the navy, and the supposition that men might be required for war service again was ignored. None of the lessons learned by Dr Lind had been applied in improving the food ration. Additionally, the seamen's pay remained as it had been a century before, and punishment had increased in severity.

There were two further cogent reasons for the massive desertion which took place in the early years of this war. For one thing, it was difficult to motivate the British seaman to fight adversaries many of whom were his own kith and kin; the cause lacked conviction in the eyes of the average British sailor. Another equally important factor was the slight rise in living and social standards ashore which brought into sharp focus the lack of similar progress afloat. In the initial stages of the war the quality of leadership did not help either, a fault which can be attributed to the fact that many officers had been placed on half-pay during the period of peace and thus had been absent from the navy for too long a period.

The entry of France into the war on the side of the American colonists changed attitudes however and provided the will and determination to resist which the backs-to-the-wall situation demanded. Officers regained the professionalism they had shown in the Seven Years war and increasingly realised the importance of caring for their men. The autocratic powers of captains could sway the efficiency and contentment of their crews from one extreme to the other. Few seamen minded a martinet provided he was fair and provided they knew where they stood from the captain's own written orders. One captain at this time — Charles Middleton, later to become First Lord of the Admiralty at the critical time of Trafalgar and inventor of what was to be known as the Divisional System in the Royal Navy — provided model orders. His system placed the responsibility on officers — to use Middleton's own words — 'to get so well acquainted with the character and disposition of their men as to be able to answer at any time such particulars as may be required concerning them'. His cure for drunkenness was novel but effective, 'If any seaman or marine gets drunk on board or on shore, he is to be taken care of till sober, and the following morning to be ordered in custody of the master-at-arms and brought upon the quarterdeck, where the purser's steward is to serve him, in the presence of the commanding officer and the ship's company, a pint of salt water which he is to drink. If drunk a second time, to be punished with six lashes; if a third time with twelve lashes; and if habitually so, to be reported to me.'

The importance at this time of the beer ration, and of rum and wine as substitutes, cannot be over estimated, although by a variety of stratagem a sailor could obtain more than was good for him. For example, men cruising in ships for days on end in vile weather conditions off Brest, Ushant or the Lizard, needed a daily pick-me-up to maintain their morale. But even when needed most, sometimes the issue was unavailable. For example, in 1779 the British fleet under Admiral Hardy, consisting of thirty ships of the line, had to keep at sea in westerly gales to counter a threat of invasion by the combined fleets of France and Spain. Operating in home waters, the British seamen were entitled only to their one gallon a day beer ration and no rum. The Admiralty assured Admiral Hardy they would keep him supplied with beer at sea so that he need not go into port. That they were slow in honouring their promise is shown by this extract from Hardy's letter to Admiralty, written onboard *HMS Victory* at Torbay on July 10, 1779, when taking temporary refuge from the weather. The *Victory* had started her active life the previous year and still had twenty-six years of service before her until that celebrated moment when she led Nelson's fleet into battle off Cape Trafalgar. Hardy's letter read, 'My Lord — I can assure you we felt ourselves very happy the night we came into this bay; for it blew so hard that night, had the fleet been in the Channel we must have been driven so far to the eastward as might have obliged me to have put into St Helen's with the fleet.

'Your lordship may be assured I shall not lose a moment's time in putting to sea. The time we have been here the ships have been fully employed in recruiting their water, but we are still without any supply of beer, though I have daily expected some from Plymouth; and as that liquor is highly necessary for preserving the men's health while at sea I have mentioned it in my public letter to the Board, for in the last war our being constantly supplied with beer and water, sent us in transports off Brest, preserved the men's health in those long cruises so much that on our returning into port we put very few men into the hospitals and buried very few at sea.'

Whether the seamen were given grog on those days at Torbay when beer was unavailable, is not on record. One fervently hopes so as even *fresh* water taken onboard would have been a poor substitute! Concerning the supply of water, there had been a minor but nevertheless significant advance, for the distillation of fresh from salt water in small quantities had been made possible by an Admiralty order of 1772 directing ships to fit themselves with a still invented by Dr Lynn. Only a token amount could be obtained by this method to which the surgeon had a prior right for the sick. The rest of the ship's company continued to draw their water from shore in cask, as some years were to pass before iron storage tanks came into use.

The area of conflict expanded with the war. Mercantile trade needed protection and both the British and French had already adopted the convoy system, but the more warlike theatres where fleets actually confronted each other were in the West Indies, the North American waters, the Indian Ocean, and off the Spanish coast. In addition to these overseas commitments the navy had to maintain an ever watchful guard in home waters.

The demand for rum for ships bound for foreign stations increased yearly while the war lasted. There was no doubting now that rum was popular and much preferred to any alternative. Stowage space aboard controlled the amount which could be carried and it was not always possible to replenish stocks when ships were away from home shores. While in foreign ports, local substitutes allowed by the regulations had to be bought. There had been no change in the 1731 formula of 'a pint of wine, or half a pint of brandy, rum or arrack, hold proportion to a gallon of beer'.

Geography dictated that wine — and sometimes brandy — was available in the Mediterranean, while arrack distilled from rice and other materials such as cocoa sap — was obtainable in far-eastern waters. Arrack had a reputation of being potent but there is no evidence to show that it appealed on board.

Understandably, too, wine — usually mediocre — was looked upon as a poor substitute for rum. Two fiery Spanish white wines called rosolio and mistela were the favourites, the latter becoming known as Miss Taylor to the seamen who, throughout history, have shown a flair for inventing nicknames. The red wine known as Black Strap was unpopular, thus being posted to the Mediterranean was meant being 'black-strapped'. Whatever the sailor's views about it, wine continued to receive Dr Blane's support for he appreciated its curative value against scurvy. 'There is no cordial equal to good wine in recruiting men who are recovering', he claimed, a sentiment that has its modern equivalent in 'Guinness is good for you'.

Nelson, too, was an enthusiast for wine although he himself was abstemious. Marsala, a popular gunroom beverage, was a cheap but drinkable Madeira-type wine, reputed to have been made popular in England by Nelson after making acquaintance with it in Sicily.

The great man's faculty for looking after his men is well known, and by placing them on a pedestal of importance he received a loyal and whole-hearted response even in the most trying times. To give but one example concerning the long blockade of the French fleet before Toulon prior to the chase to the West Indies and the *coup de grâce* at Trafalgar. This was a protracted affair made bearable only by exceptional leadership and understanding. It is said that in his devotion to duty Nelson did not step ashore from his flagship for more than two years, and certainly that would have been true of the majority of his crew. On March 11, 1804, Nelson wrote from *HMS Victory*, 'It is easier for an officer to keep men healthy than for a physician to cure them. Situated as this fleet has been, without a friendly port, where we could get all the things so necessary for us, yet I have, by changing the cruizing ground, not allowed the same-ness of prospect to satiate the mind — sometimes by looking at Toulon, Ville Franche, Barcelona and Rosas; then running round

Minorca, Majorca, Sardinia and Corsica; and two or three times anchoring for a few days, and sending a ship to the last place for onions, which I find the best thing that can be given to seamen; having always good mutton for the sick, cattle when we can get them, and plenty of fresh water. In the winter it is the best plan to give half the allowance of grog, instead of all wine. These things are for the Commander-in-Chief to look to; but shut very nearly out from Spain, and only getting refreshments by stealth from other places, my command has been an arduous one. Our men's minds are always kept up with the daily hopes of meeting the enemy.'

Nelson echoes Rodney's sentiments that rum is preferable in cold or adverse weather, but the letter also shows clearly that the commander-in-chief of those days had wide and flexible powers at his disposal even greater than those available to individual captains.

There is little to record on rum's other substitutes, brandy and arrack. It was a minor scandal that, until the Treaty of Amiens in 1802, the British navy even in wartime was supplied contractually with brandy by French merchants. 'At last,' so it is recorded, 'John Bull awoke from his dream, and it struck him that soldiers and sailors liked rum just as well as brandy, which would not only assist the West Indian merchants, but give general satisfaction throughout the fleet.'

Arrack was consumed only when other liquors had been exhausted. References to it are few but the crew of the *Pandora* sent to the Pacific to recover the mutineers of the *Bounty*, were given two drams per day of arrack after the sinking of their ship in the Torres Strait. It is also on record that arrack was served at times in the *Resolution* during Captain James Cook's second voyage of discovery to the Pacific.

Recipes for palatable drinks from available ingredients were sometimes devised. The accounts of Cook's voyages are full of examples. A beverage similar to spruce beer was made aboard the *Resolution* from ingredients obtained at the Cape of Good Hope. According to custom, it replaced the spirit issue while available. By adding a small amount of rum and brown sugar to the beer, it was found to provide a pleasantly refreshing and healthy drink. When stirred vigorously it tasted — so the report says — 'rather like champagne, and was called Kallebogas after a similar mixture in North America'. The North American recipes according to one ship's journal were, 'Spruce beer with rum, or brandy, or gin added made Callibogus, with egg and sugar, made Egg Calli; with spirits drunk hot, made King's Calli'.

Hot champagne sounds, if nothing else, rather daunting!

But there were dangers of drinking to excess. One instance is told of two Royal Marines at Halifax swilling Calibolus (the variations of spelling are as given), and then drinking three pints of neat rum. Both died. Drunkenness was ever a problem in the navy. During the Revolutionary and Napoleonic wars it reached such unacceptable proportions as to become a menace. Certainly it was caused by an over-generous spirit ration at sea; but the ease with which wine and spirit were smuggled aboard in harbour also aggravated the problem. Enlightened senior officers were beginning to realise the need to reduce its incidence but as will be seen, while the war was still being fought, the feeling — probably rightly — was to leave well alone.

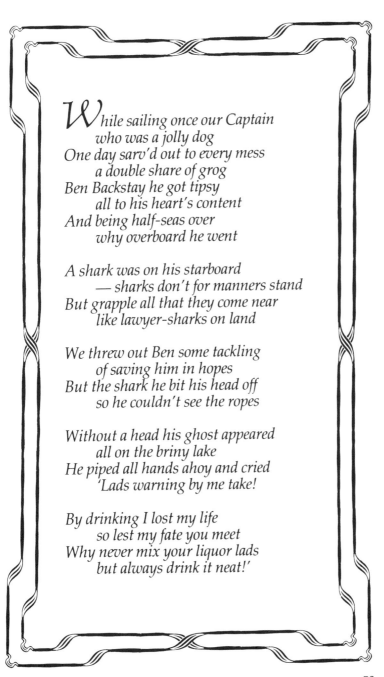

*W*hile sailing once our Captain
    who was a jolly dog
One day sarv'd out to every mess
    a double share of grog
Ben Backstay he got tipsy
    all to his heart's content
And being half-seas over
    why overboard he went

A shark was on his starboard
    — sharks don't for manners stand
But grapple all that they come near
    like lawyer-sharks on land

We threw out Ben some tackling
    of saving him in hopes
But the shark he bit his head off
    so he couldn't see the ropes

Without a head his ghost appeared
    all on the briny lake
He piped all hands ahoy and cried
    'Lads warning by me take!

By drinking I lost my life
    so lest my fate you meet
Why never mix your liquor lads
    but always drink it neat!'

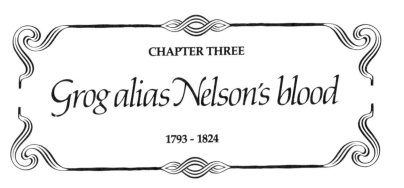

BEN BACKSTAY'S FATE may seem over-exaggerated for the sake of an amusing piece of doggerel, but it bears comparison with an entry in Captain Cook's log on his first voyage during which he charted the coasts of New Zealand and eastern Australia: *HMS Endeavour*, Monday, August 28, . . . departed this life Jno Radon, boatswain's mate, his death was occasioned by the boatswain, out of mere good nature, giving him part of a bottle of rum last night; which it is supposed he drank all at once; he was found to be very much in liquor last night, but this was no more than what was common with him when he could get any, no further notice was taken of him then to put him to bed when this morning about eight o'clock he was found speechless and past recovery.'

No evidence points to any serious enquiry into the events leading to this man's death or to any punishment meted out to the boatswain for his 'good nature'. Perhaps there was good reason for turning the proverbial blind eye, although the celebrated botanist Sir Joseph Banks accompanying Cook on this voyage, and thus able to take a detached view, makes this indictable comment, 'One of the seamen Rayden by name (his spelling), was this morn found so drunk that he had scarce any signs of life and in about an hour he expired. Where he could have got his liquor is a mystery which however, nobody seems to enquire into probably not fairly. . . .'

It is easy to overlook the fact that officers were also entitled to the daily allowance of rum so that any irregularity in its issue or receipt could involve them no less than any other member of the ship's company — and frequently did. Even chaplains could discredit their cloth in the search for rum, and one account records, 'Our old parson was a "rum" subject. After trying all other mess places he got old Pipes, the boatswain, to take him into his. They agreed very well for a little while; but one unfortunate day, the evil genius of poor old Fritz prevailed, for Pipes coming down rather unexpectedly to his cabin in the fore cockpit to get a glass of grog, having got wet when the hands were turned up reefing topsails, found the parson helping himself rather too freely out of his liquor-case. This was a crime the boatswain could not tolerate. A breach immediately ensued, and an instant dismissal from his berth took place with the exclamation of, "The parson is such a black; I cannot allow him to mess with me any longer." After this occurrence the captain interfered, and he again messed in his proper place with the officers in the wardroom.'

Commissioned officers had servants who, on one pretext or another, would have had access to most corners of the ship, and whose abilities to procure for their masters would have been highly developed. Could the answer have been therefore, in the sad demise of Jonathan Radon aboard the *Endeavour*, that it was considered diplomatic to let sleeping dogs lie and not to probe too deeply into an event which might show improper practices on the part of an officer? The fact that the *Endeavour* was a small ship — a converted east coast collier — and that she was the independent command of James Cook thousands of miles away from enquiring authority, might also have had some bearing.

If liquor was an ever-present temptation in a minor war vessel as Cook's journals amply show, it must have been a problem of enormous magnitude in a ship of the line, where a ship's company exceeded eight hundred souls. Dividing the grog ration into a morning and evening issue, as had been the practice since Vernon's day, was with the laudable object of spreading the intake. But those seamen who wanted to were never at a loss in devising a way of saving the morning ration to add to the evening one. Also, as grog was ever an instrument for barter, it was not too difficult for an individual to have his flowing bowl in the evening by arrangement with a messmate. Unfortunately this was the time of the day when men were most vulnerable. Immediately after supper, the normal routine was to exercise at stations under the close scrutiny of the officers in attendance. Rather like a bird of prey, the master-at-arms would be hovering to select his victims for the kill. Many who had supplemented their evening grog would be at his mercy, and even the innocent were at times taken into custody and flogged. The harsh discipline of the time allowed little excuse, no matter how plausible, and the legions who perhaps deserved the cat-of-nine tails, included the occasional Billy Budd whose good fortune had deserted him.

It is scant wonder then that drunkenness had become an occupational disorder of alarming magnitude. The press gang had literally scraped the barrel and, to make up the numbers required, Parliament had introduced the Quota Acts under which English counties and the larger towns were called upon to provide men in proportion to their population. Known as Lord Mayor's men for the simple reason that the majority were drafted into the navy in lieu of a prison sentence, they were unpromising material. Nor could they be seamen in the true sense. Entered under the title of 'landsmen' they tended to be the butt of the true seamen, although adequate for the routine duties assigned to them. Their diverse, often unsatisfactory, backgrounds were utilised as well as they could by the naval system at a time when revolution was in the air. Even after the Spithead and Nore mutinies there was an aftermath of discontent in most ships, created in the main by Voltaireans with political motives. Firm but benevolent leadership provided the best remedy and reaped a generous response. For example, shortly after Nelson joined *HMS Theseus*, a potentially mutinous ship during this period, he received a note, discovered on the quarterdeck, 'Success attend Admiral Nelson. God bless Captain Miller. We thank them for the officers they have placed over us. We are happy and comfortable, and will shed every drop of blood in our veins, and the name of the *Theseus* shall be immortalised as high as the Captain's. — Signed by the Ship's Company,'

The spirit ration contributed more to a state of equilibrium than might be imagined. Grog times — morning and evening — were the pleasantest parts of the day, and provided the anodyne to counteract the miseries and discomfort of life aboard. It was the link of the spirit ration with excessive punishment which gave rum such a bad name.

Admiral Lord St Vincent, a leader much admired by Nelson himself, provided the best answer — a palliative but not a cure. He made it a rule, in the fleet which he commanded off Cadiz at this time, that men were never to be punished after the serving of evening grog, saying, 'that as punishments more frequently occur with the evening's duties, the natural inference is that by the freer circulation of the glass on such occasions, some of the party become heated and irritable.' St Vincent's order was intended for officers no less than for the men. In a manner similar to Charles Middleton, (Chapter two), he made his officers responsible for the maintenance of calm and a sense of proportion. St Vincent showed an equal concern for the men's welfare in harbour, placing the onus once again upon the officers by telling them that they 'must not leave them to their own devices'.

Shore leave for ships' crews still remained a pipe dream; no answer had been found to the general debauchery which filled the seamen's leisure hours under harbour routine. No sooner was a ship anchored than the bumboatmen surrounded her and offloaded their human cargo and illicit wares. After the fair sex, raw liquor was probably next in demand and there was no shortage of purveyors. A novel punishment, sometimes applied to a bumboatman caught in the act of smuggling spirits aboard, was to hoist him and his boat to the main yardarm and leave him there to reflect upon his sins, but this was a mild penance compared with floggings and other indignities suffered by the seamen under the Articles of War.

A word on punishment at this period which shows how unjust it could be, comes from the anonymous sailor of the period, Jack Nastyface, 'It is generally supposed that no man could be punished without having been guilty of some serious offence; but that is not always the case, for nineteen out of twenty men that are punished suffer without being conscious that they have violated any law, and in many instances they are the most expert and able seamen. For instance, the fore, main, and mizen-top men are selected from the crew as the most sprightly and attentive to their duty; and yet those men are more frequently punished, and are always in dread when aloft lest they should be found fault with for not being quick enough, for punishment is sure to follow, and sure enough, their conjectures are generally too true; for they are not only flogged, but their grog is stopped, or compelled to drink six or eight water grog for a length of time.'

Despite this tyranny, the British tar won six conclusive victories within eleven years at The Glorious First of June, St Vincent, Camperdown, The Nile, Copenhagen and Trafalgar. It could not all have been bad!

Admiral Lord St Vincent as an old man. He ordered that men were never to be punished after the evening issue of grog

Towards the end of the Napoleonic wars, many senior naval officers became increasingly aware of the direct relationship between drunkenness and punishment, and urged the Admiralty to reduce the spirit ration. Their Lordships preferred to follow a policy of 'ne pas reveiller le chat qui dort'. They knew that living conditions could not be ameliorated, thus in their opinion to reduce rum without compensation was simply courting trouble. It was amoral, of course, to do nothing when confronted with so obvious an evil, but to be fair the administrative detail of communicating a decision would have been enormous by today's standards. Despatches took an age to arrive on a foreign station and sometimes did not arrive at all. Who, in their right senses, would reduce rum in wartime and in these circumstances? Men have mutinied for less!

Admiral Lord Keith, a sagacious officer of wide sea experience, was perhaps the leading exponent for a reduction in rum. On this subject he wrote to their lordships on September 1, 1812,

'San Josef, off Ushant
Sir, In performing the important duty of bringing before their lordships' attention the number and extent of punishments that occur in the squadron under my orders, it is observable and deeply to be lamented that almost every crime except theft originates in drunkenness, and that a large proportion of the men who are maimed and disabled are reduced to that situation by accidents that happen from the same abominable vice.

'It is an evil of great magnitude, and one which it will be impossible to prevent so long as the present excessive quantity

of spirits is issued in the Royal Navy; for men seem to have no othe idea of the use of spirits than as they afford them the means of running into excess and indulging in intoxication. There is a great difference between a ship's company in a morning and an afternoon as there can possibly be; for although their spirits are mixed with four times the quantity of water and issued at two separate periods of the day sufficiently distant from each other, yet not only young and raw lads from the country but the more crafty and experienced, who contrive to purchase or cheat their messmates, are often so drunk as to be insensible of the most severe fractures by falls, or even of having fallen overboard when under the influence of drink.

'It is at all times a delicate point to interfere with what is called an allowance or right, and the present may not be the moment for reforming even so great an evil; but in the event of peace I am

The delegates of the Nore mutiny in council 1797. This mutiny had political and revolutionary undertones fortunately absent from the Spithead Mutiny in the same year.
Note the man on the extreme right is pouring grog into his can

Admiral Lord Keith who advocated a reduction in the rum ration

satisfied that not a more essential service could be rendered to the nation than to reduce the quantity of spirits now used in the navy; and I am convinced that such will be general opinion of all the officers in the service if their lordships are pleased to require their sentiments on the subject.

'I beg you will be pleased to assure their lordships that it is not from any officiousness of disposition that I have ventured to submit my opinion upon the matter, but because I consider it to be an act of duty imperiously called for.

Keith'

No action was taken and on November 18, 1813, Keith returned to the charge with another letter to Admiralty,

'*Hannibal,* Cawsand Bay,

Sir, In reference to their lordships' directions of the 16th inst, on the stoppage of grog on board the *Ville de Paris,* I beg to observe that, as the constant source of punishment was drunkenness and flogging seemed to have lost its effect, I recommended other means, such as additional duties, disgrace etc, and that of throwing the grog of those habitual drunkards who infest every ship into the sea before their faces; and it has been found that this practice has produced good effects. In no ship, I believe, are spirits mixed with less than five of water, nor the grog served out less than twice daily, after dinner and before sunset; yet the crime of drunkenness continues to prevail. In fact the quantity of spirits is too much. Although the quantity of water in some ships has been increased in mixing the grog, it gave rise to complaint from the more discreet part of the ships' companies and in some instances a refusal to take it.

'That it is a delicate point to interfere, I readily admit; and I shall therefore at all times feel great consolation from their lordships' instructions and cause them to be strictly attended to.

Keith'

It is noteworthy that in letters written with an interval of a year or so between them, the identical words, 'it is a delicate point to interfere . . .' appear. Poor Keith has been accused by historians of showing lack of courage, and perhaps his letters do not possess what is commonly known as 'the Nelson touch', but the proposal certainly bristled with difficulties in wartime. After all, the war was being won and peace was not far away — less than two years in fact to the victory at Waterloo which settled all. Keith was right to introduce a note of caution. It may be added that before this culminating victory, the English troops had been given an issue of spirits. After the battle and the enemy's hurried retreat, the Emperor's abandoned carriage was captured and an unopened bottle of rum — not brandy — was discovered.

With peace, the navy was reduced to a fraction of its wartime size; 145,000 men became 25,000 in very little time, causing no particular problems for the Admiralty who simply discharged all

A lower gun deck scene on board a man-of-war in harbour during the Napoleonic Wars. The long sweep of this deck allowed no privacy

conscripts as ships entered port to be paid off. The end of the commission was that moment when seamen received the final settlement of their pay accounts — hence the term 'paid off'.

Their Lordships now had no difficulty in manning those ships which remained on active service as, naturally enough, there was an abundance of men seeking employment. The wars had given Britain supremacy of the seas and with no challengers on the horizon there was no longer a need for a large navy. All the same, the appellation of Mistress of the Seas hardly seemed apposite to the run-down force she now had. An unfortunate side effect was that many officers who had become promising material for higher rank in wartime, now had no incentive and quit on half-pay. Those that remained were mostly prepared to accept the slow promotion which waiting for dead-men's shoes

entailed, and so their quality fell.

None of these circumstances helped to accelerate badly-needed reform, and Keith's proposals of an earlier year to reduce the rum ration as soon as the peace came continued to be shelved. In short, the navy was back to the familiar war-peace syndrome.

Drunkenness, far from becoming less of a problem, developed even more as the curse of the service. The old habit of smuggling liquor aboard worsened as seamen could now take occasional leave to frequent shoreside taverns.

Finally, in 1823, the Admiralty decided to act and selected *HMS Thetis* under the command of Captain Sir John Phillimore as a trial ship for a number of proposed changes, including a reduction in the spirit ration. The daily rum issue was halved to a quarter of a pint (a gill), and in compensation tea and cocoa were issued, and two shillings per month added to the men's pay. The reaction which Keith feared, 'it is a delicate point to interfere' as he put it, was not slow in coming. He was right after all! Other ships' companies looked upon men of the *Thetis* as stool-pigeons and gave them a rough time. Then a fortunate event occurred — the enlightened crew of *HMS Ganges* — a second-rate ship of the line which had just returned from foreign service — gave their support in favour of the trial continuing. There was no further trouble.

The experiment was deemed successful and when the changes were permanently introduced in the following year (1824), they included a bonus, an increased meat ration. This was significant progress since from early times the navy had had its meatless, or Banyan days (from a name derived from Hindu sources), and the abolition of these represented a real advance in messing standards. Accompanying these important changes was the decision to restrict grog to the noonday issue and to do away with its evening equivalent. St Vincent and Keith had won, at least for the time being.

Greenwich pensioners overcoming the handicap of lost limbs

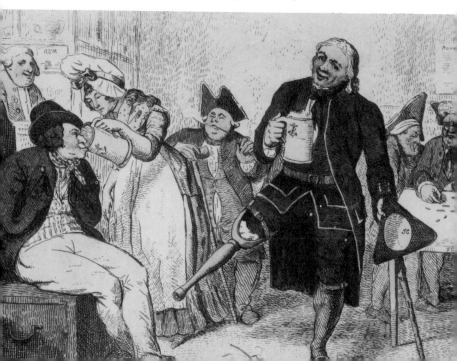

*T*hen trust me there's
nothing like drinking
So pleasant on this side
of the grave
It keeps the unhappy
from thinking
And makes e'en the valiant
more brave

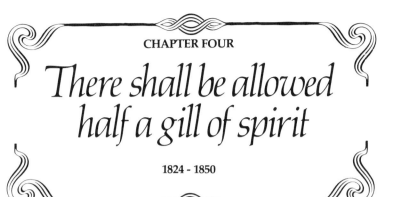

CHAPTER FOUR

There shall be allowed half a gill of spirit

1824 - 1850

BY REDUCING THE RATION of rum to a gill, the Board of Admiralty may have felt that they had scotched drunkenness. But a gill then was equal in strength to at least four double whiskies today and even as grog, was still a potent mixture. Looking back, however, there is nothing to suggest that Their Lordships applied themselves to the problem with reforming zeal for in 1824 the new imperial gallon was introduced, the effect of which was to add one fifth to the rum ration, neutralising much of the benefit gained from the recent reduction. Evidence suggests the change-over was regarded as a minor detail, so on this basis why should Their Lordships interfere again with the seaman's inalienable right? To make matters worse, however, they allowed the evening issue to be reintroduced, presumably in order to spread the increased ration. Keith who had protested so vehemently against it must have turned in his grave!

The navy was living through a period of neglect during which the government faced the perplexing task of economic reconstruction. Supremacy at sea had sustained a flourishing overseas trade, which in turn nourished the industrial revolution now under way.

The country's major problem was how to overcome growing discontent. Cause and effect boomeranged on the navy. Steam engines provided a new source of power in factories and foundries, but their adaptation for ship propulsion was still a long way off. The British bluejacket had served his country well in the Great Wars, but his value had now depreciated and was to remain thus until well into the latter half of the nineteenth century. The fact that the navy had many officers who were inefficient, unimaginative and ripe for superannuation, added to the problem of resistance to change or to experiment. When the seamen's services were urgently required again in a national crisis, as always, the story would be different. All the same, despite few visible changes for the better, subtle improvements were indeed taking place. William the Fourth, affectionately known as the Sailor King because of his earlier service in the navy, came to the throne in 1830. During his reign, service victualling became more professional.

Mention has been made of the important change in 1832 which brought the victualling commissioners directly under the jurisdiction of the Admiralty Board, and it was at about the same time that two new victualling yards were built at Gosport and Devonport to supplement the main yard at Deptford. Apart from containing buildings of great architectural merit and elegance, the Royal Clarence Yard at Gosport, and the Royal William Yard at Devonport (both named in honour of the King), incorporated up-to-date facilities ranging from biscuit-making and slaughter-houses for providing meat, to vats for the stowage and supply of rum, all on a scale never before attempted.

Records reveal that the exclusive brokering rights for supplying rum to the Royal Navy started in 1784 when they were awarded to James Man, a cooper and merchant dealing in a variety of goods imported from the West Indies. The rum, obtained by the broker at about 40% overproof, was delivered to a bonded warehouse from which it was bought by the victualling department. The department then arranged with the Customs and Excise for the rum to be transferred to the Deptford vats, and later to Gosport and Devonport vats where it was reduced in strength for supply to ships in cask. The Admiralty must have had a high opinion of James Man, for the family continued to supply rum under this valued contract for nearly two hundred years. In 1870, when the laws of England permitted the registration of a business name, the firm was registered as E D and F Man, taking the initials of the then current partners. The company's name remains unchanged to this day.

The 'proof' of spirit which in earlier days could be assessed only by rule-of-thumb, was established far more accurately after 1818 by an Act of Parliament which adopted the Sikes's hydrometer measurement for revenue purposes. Sikes's invention provided a reliable way of determining proof strength by taking hydrometer readings and converting them to per cent alcohol by the use of prepared tables. The Inland Revenue could now assess the duty payable on spirit according to its proof — which was defined as a mixture of 49.24% alcohol and 50.76% water by weight.

So within two decades after the ending of the wars, great progress had been made technically in the supply of rum. This provided an organisation much more able to cope efficiently with fleet requirements. Coupled with this, the navy was the Revenue's friend in the war against smuggling, and for this reason was able to obtain preferential duty-free privileges.

Even harbour ships, classified as 'In Ordinary' (in reserve in modern parlance), were commissioned as stationary guardships and given the duty-free government stores and groceries which previously had been the preserve of commissioned vessels proceeding abroad.

Another change, in 1831, heralded the coming of age of rum as part of the seamen's daily ration for in that year the general issue of beer to the fleet was terminated. Beer had had a long run, spanning hundreds of years from the time of the Armada. Its withdrawal was for sound enough reasons — doubtful storage qualities, shortages when it was needed, and most of all the problem of providing sufficient stowage space onboard. Now, in the nineteenth century, it could not even justify its need on the grounds of its anti-scorbutic qualities and, in any case, there standing in the wings was rum — well matured, acceptable to most seamen, and cheap.

However, beer continued to be brewed in the victualling yard brewhouses for another twenty years providing for the sick in naval hospitals and infirmaries. Indeed, as late as 1870, it was still aboard troop transports as 'medical comforts'.

The navy's bible, *The Regulations and Instructions Relating to His Majesty's Service at Sea,* was slow to react to change. Nevertheless, it is possible to detect sundry nuances through each succeeding set of regulations. For example, in 1820 orders were still in force that lemon juice and sugar were to be mixed with grog on foreign stations. Five years later the regulations no longer included such provision, presumably because by that time anti-scorbutic measures in the dietary system were better understood.

A glaring example of official failure to catch up with events occurred in the 1833 regulations, two years after the beer issue had ceased. Following the usual proviso about 'no drams', the regulation went on, 'When spirit is issued in place of beer, the captain is strictly enjoined to cause the allowance for the ship's company to be mixed every day. . . .' This must have been difficult to implement when there was no longer any beer to replace!

On the other hand there were frequent clauses which suggested that the security of rum stocks was now Their Lordships' major concern. Thus an order in 1820 directed to the purser read, 'As there are proper and convenient places set apart in the hold for securing spirits and wine from any abuses, and which are not to be applied to any other purpose whatever, he is to take care that casks containing these liquors be sound and full at the time of their coming onboard, and that they are lodged in the places appropriated for them, as he will be answerable for keeping them afterwards and must not expect to be allowed any claim for leakage thereon.' One wonders who was the villain; the purser or others with outstanding thirsts? Nor does the captain escape injunction in the 1833 regulations. Thus, 'Orders for Captains — He is moreover most strictly enjoined never, on any account or pretence, to allow spirituous liquors to be drawn off, or moved from one cask or vessel to another, anywhere but on the upper deck by daylight, except in case of emergency at night; to provide for which a small cask is always to be kept at hand in the spirit room to be got upon deck, and the lights necessary on such an occasion are to be secured in good lanterns, and kept as far from the spirits as possible; and when a spirit cask is emptied, a quantity of salt water is immediately to be poured into it.' In this instance it is difficult to assess whether Their Lordships were concerned with the possibility of the captain blowing up his ship in dealing carelessly with volatile rum, or whether it is directed at 'bulling' — the practice of putting a small quantity of fresh water into an empty rum cask and leaving it until it became grog.

A distinctly peevish note entered a memorandum on the Extra Issue of Spirits dated September 15, 1835, which stated, 'The Lords Commissioners having noticed the numerous claims in the accounts of the pursers of HM Ships for extra issues of spirits . . . such issues will never be allowed unless in cases of extraordinary and unavoidable exposure or fatigue, and even then the recommendation of the surgeon should accompany the usual certificate.'

Rum started its reign at about the same time as Queen Victoria began hers. By 1837, the system of receiving, stowing and issuing it was far more organised. Virtually it had been recognised *de facto* as part of the daily victualling ration which meant that the crews of all ships in commission — including officers — were entitled to draw their tot regularly, and resort to substitutes were infrequent. Grog, in fact, was about to celebrate its centenary, its popularity firmly established. In 1844, the daily ration was prescribed as a gill (a quarter pint Imperial), at which point rum had probably reached its apogee. Its gradual descent can be traced from this time, and, in quantitative terms, the daily ration of a quarter of an Imperial, was never to be exceeded again.

Rum now ruled supreme; beer virtually had withdrawn from the league but wine maintained a position towards the lower end of the table, greatly helped in its efforts to avoid relegation by the award in 1793 of duty-free status. In that year an act empowered commissioned officers in command to obtain wines duty-free, and all ships proceeding on foreign service took wine aboard for issue as a substitute when necessary. By the present-day standards the quantities allowed to each officer — rank by rank — were ridiculously liberal.

'Wines of any sort provided the total quantity per annum does not exceed:

For an Admiral	6 tons (1260 gallons)
Vice Admiral	5 tons
Rear Admiral	4 tons
Captain 1st/2nd rates	3 tons
Captain 3rd/4th/5th rates	2 tons
Captain below 5th rate	1 ton
Lieutenant and other commissioned officers	½ ton'

Wine also found favour as a medical comfort for which an extra allowance was made under the care of the surgeon. There was much sense in treating wine as duty-free, as history showed. For instance, Lord Dundonald when captain of the *Pallas* had captured a considerable number of chasse-marées, some laden with the finest clarets. After giving a liberal supply to Admiral Thornborough's squadron there still remained a large stock which the victualling board, for some inscrutable reason, declined to take over even at the price of the small beer of the day. To avoid Custom's dues, the wine was tipped overboard (excepting a small quantity reserved by Lord Dundonald for his personal friends)!

With rum ascendant and all ships embarking it upon commissioning, brandy was displaced, and as for arrack — the far eastern substitute of the previous century — little more was heard of it.

By the 1840's the navy was carrying out its many overseas commitments with distinction despite a shortage of manpower. Few seamen could truly be called volunteers even though the Impress Service had died quietly and unmourned in 1833. Ships were now manned through a Register of Seamen which rendered men liable to five years' naval service when their names came forward so that integrating landmen was no longer the problem it had been in earlier wars.

The service seamen were expected to undertake was wide and varied, invariably demanding endurance, adaptability, and high courage. In China, the bluejacket was faced by a doughty and unorthodox opponent ashore; in New Zealand by the warlike Maoris; off the west coast of Africa by ruthless slave traders; in Borneo by raiding pirates; and in the Arctic by impenetrable ice.

Living conditions could improve but little so long as wooden ships under sail were the order of the day, for their internal construction made radical change difficult. The gundeck was still the messdeck where men ate, fought, slept and spent their leisure. Hammocks were slung with scarcely twenty inches between them, thus preventing circulation of air. In consequence, the atmosphere was usually hot and humid, sometimes toxic when mixed with the vapours which rose from the ship's hold.

By this time, water was no longer supplied in cask as iron tanks had been fitted in most ships. This was an improvement but another decade was to pass before distilling apparatus, providing pure water, became available generally. Most ships now had sick bays on the upper deck under the forecastle which represented a great advance on the *ad hoc* arrangements of earlier days, but in action the orlop deck was used still as a casualty station. Cleanliness and other aids to hygiene were now strictly observed in the sick berth, and medical comforts were supplied far more liberally.

The preservation of meat and soups also advanced, and the fleet responded enthusiastically to the introduction of 'bully beef' — derived from the *boeuf bouilli* of the French navy where it was already tried and proven. These new methods improved the general diet, although the seaman's innate antipathy to change, when it came to food, still tended to resist dietary reform. However, greater resort to fresh vegetables, when obtainable, helped to reduce scurvy to the isolated outbreak.

The daily rum ration at a quarter of a pint per day, quite demonstrably, was still too much. Ironically, the extra tea and sugar, which seamen were allowed, was a frequent cause of the evening issue of grog being given away by a man to his friend. 'Rum Rats' (the name for those whose unquenchable thirst gave them a highly developed olfaction for the spirit), collected extra supplies in this way. There is one recorded instance where the cook of the mess received the grog of thirty-two men! It was far too easy in the early Victorian navy for anyone with a taste for rum to obtain more than was good for him. Indeed, the entire procedure of supply, stowage and issue in wooden walled ships offered a security problem which was largely to disappear in later years when it became possible in the ship's design to incorporate separate storage spaces, and to make special provision for a spirit room.

John Bechervaise — a Channel Islander who served in the Victorian navy — had this to say about grog in his auto-biography of lower decklife, 'The man who wrote these lines would not drink one glass of ardent spirits though the empty glass was to be given him full of sovereigns. The many punish-ments I saw inflicted on my first joining the service, for crimes committed in drunkenness, induced me to say, that I, never while I breathe, would taste spirits, and thousands of circumstances have tended to confirm my resolution.' He commented favourably on the effects of the halving of the rum ration in 1824 by saying that were the logs of two identical ships to be compared for similar periods pre-1824 and post-1824, the number of lashes inflicted for the first period would be shown to be far more than double the later period. He confirms the relationship between drinking and punishment by observing, 'Examine the log of a ship of the present time (1839), after having been three years in commission, and it will be found that one half the punishment inflicted has been for excessive drinking or neglect or error caused by it.'

Both drunkenness and flogging were still problems of the utmost gravity and it is doubtful whether the 1824 halving the rum issue to a quarter of a pint of rum had any long-lasting effect regardless of what Bechervaise may have thought.

In 1835 a Royal Commission gave its views on punishment, but although public and even naval reaction to flogging was gaining ground, it was many years before Admiralty responded to these pressures. Flogging continued to be the main occupational hazard of the navy, and sentences could descend upon the unsuspecting — and frequently the undeserving — with the suddenness and horror of the *auto-da-fé*. Yet because of the brutishness of lower deck life flogging sometimes had a prestige value — a machismo, particularly with younger sailors who wished to show that they could take their punishment like men. Variants of the whipping game, though not as severe, were symptomatic of the same disease. One such was known as 'to marry the gunner's daughter' — usually reserved for boys' minor misdemeanours, and involving a thrashing while secured to the breech of a gun.

There were no common standards of punishment. A man could return to his ship from shore senseless with drink and be left to sleep it off. Provided he was fit enough to turn to and work with the hands in the morning, no more would be said. At the other extreme, a taut captain would not demur from 'scratching a man's back' as it was called, by ordering several dozen lashes even though officially he could award only a maximum of twelve. Captain Charles Napier, a dashing leader and a charismatic personality who rose high in the navy, had the reputation of awarding two or three dozen lashes for the first offence of drunkenness, and four dozen for a second. Even so, his ship *HMS Powerful* which played a distinguished part in the bombardment of St Jean d'Acre in 1840, was not an unhappy ship by the standards of that time.

Again the realisation was growing that the daily rum ration was excessive, and the sequence of events bears similarity to those preceding the 1824 reduction. One attempted remedy was known as 'drinking at the tub' which, as the title implies, required the men to draw and drink their grog under official gaze. Normally the cooks of the mess conveyed the appropriate number of rations to the lower deck, but under the new system the ship's company mustered by the tub and drank their grog there in turn. It was successful in reducing drunkenness but had the disadvantage of being time-consuming, particularly in larger ships, and was unpopular with the seamen who must have disliked surveillance of their most precious moment of the day. It also interfered with dinner time, and rapidly became a form of punishment. However, the grog tub itself found a place of honour in the naval ritual. Since it was required that men should doff their headgear in respect to the King when receiving their grog at the tub, the tub itself was embellished with the words, 'The King God Bless Him', and from that time onwards the practice of so lettering the tub has continued.

Pressure was mounting again for the daily rum ration to be reduced, and for that hardy annual — the evening ration — to be reviewed once more. Nearly forty years had passed since Keith had condemned it, and the reasons for abandoning it a second time were just as compelling. The Admiralty decided to appoint a Grog Committee to investigate. The results of their labours were published in 1850, a wide-ranging report which involved taking evidence from a diverse body of people, including an American naval captain, a doctor of medicine and a university professor, plus forty-eight Royal Naval officers. Why the opinion of the American was sought is not known, but it shows that a close relationship between the two navies existed and that past frictions had been forgotten. This harmonious and special friendship has continued almost uninterrupted to the present day.

The committee was quick to acknowledge that corporal punishment had proved ineffectual as a cure for drunkenness which, the seamen themselves readily admitted, was the cause of almost every crime and its resultant punishment.

The more important conclusions of the committee were, 'That the present allowance of spirits or wine be reduced by one half', and 'that the remaining portion be issued at dinner time.'

The committee members must have realised that these two recommendations by themselves would cause strong opposition so they added the compensatory clauses.

'. . . a compensation payment in money of 3s 6d
per man per calendar month.'
'That men wishing to give up the reduced allowance
shall receive a further compensation.'
'That no raw spirits be issued to anyone, except under
special circumstances, at the discretion of the Captain.'
'That provisions be brought under review, for the
purpose of a more satisfactory adjustment of the scale.'

These, and the many other proposals, were, without
question, wise and timely and, to their credit promptly
implemented by the Admiralty. For officers they heralded the
eventual withdrawal of all rum privileges; not only did they have
their ration halved but they were denied the compensatory
money allowance awarded to the men. 'No raw spirits', one
feels, was primarily directed at officers who, unlike the men, did
not receive their ration at the grog tub. Whether it was observed,
other than in the breech, is doubtful.

The Admiralty Circular was issued on October 1, 1850 with
orders that its provisions should take effect from January following, and read,

NEW SCALE OF PAY AND PROVISIONS

*By the Commissioners for Executing the Office of Lord High Admiral of the United Kingdom
of Great Britain and Ireland, & c.*

Her Majesty having been graciously pleased, with the view of improving the
condition of the Petty Officers, Seamen, and Marines, of the Fleet, to direct that the
following alterations should be made in the Scale of Victualling and Pay, of the
Royal Navy, viz

1st The allowance of Salt Meat to be increased from three-quarters of a pound, to a
pound, per man, per day.
2nd The allowance of Sugar to be likewise increased; and Mustard and Pepper to be
substituted for a certain portion of Oatmeal and Vinegar.
3rd The allowance of Spirits to be reduced; and a compensation in money to be
granted for such reduction, as shewn in the annexed Scale.
4th The Pay of the Navy to be re-cast at a daily Rate, and the compensation above
mentioned to be blended with, and form part of the Pay.
5th The Calendar to be substituted for the Lunar Month in the Payment of Wages.

You are hereby required and directed to cause the said new Scale of Victualling and
Pay, together with the Regulations attached thereto, to be promulgated, and carried
into effect, accordingly, on board Her Majesty's Ships under your command, on,
and after the 1st of January next.
In the event of any Ships of your Squadron being on a distant part of the Station,

and unable therefore to commence the new Scale of Pay and Provisions on the 1st of January next, the same to be postponed till the 1st of April following.
The necessary supply of the new Rate Books will be forwarded to you by the Storekeeper General.

Given under our hands, this 1st day of October 1850.

F T BARING	H STEWART
J W D DUNDAS	A MILNE
M F F BERKELEY	W COWPER

By Command of their Lordships,

To all Commanders-in-Chief, Captains, Commanders,   J PARKER
   and Commanding Officers of Her Majesty's Ships, and Vessels.

Table shewing the allowance of Grog and Compensation Money

RANK	Allowance of Grog	Compensation Allowance
1st Admirals, Captains, Lieutenants and Wardroom Officers	Half present allowance	Nil
2nd Mates, Assistant Surgeons, Second Master, and Clerks	Half present allowance	Savings price, for half allowance
3rd Midshipmen, Master Assistants, Clerks Assistant, and Boys of 1st Class	Do at the discretion of the Capt	Do
4th Cadets, & Boys of 2nd Class	Nil	Savings price, for whole
5th Assis Engineers, Warrant Officers, Petty Officers, Able Seamen, & others of that class, Ordinary Seamen, Non-Com. Officers and Privates of Royal Marines	Half present allowance	3s 6d per man per calendar month
6th Second Class Ord Seamen, Landsmen, and other of that Class	Half present allowance	2s 6d per man per calendar month

A Scheme of Victualling for the Navy

(Sanctioned by Her Majesty's Order in Council of the 24th September, 1850)

There shall be allowed to every person serving in Her Majesty's Navy, the following daily quantities of Provisions, viz: Biscuit 1lb, Spirits ½ gill, Fresh Meat 1lb, Vegetables ½lb, Sugar 1¾oz, Chocolate 1oz, Tea ¼oz.

When Fresh Meat and Vegetables cannot be issued, there shall be allowed in lieu thereof: Salt Pork 1lb, Peas ½ pint every alternate day; or, Salt Beef 1lb, Flour ¾ lb, or, Preserved Meat ¾lb, Preserved Potato or Rice, (or ½ of each,) ¼lb, alternately on the days when Salt Pork and Peas are not issued.

And weekly, whether Fresh, or Salt, or Preserved Meat be issued: Oatmeal ¼ pint, Mustard ½ oz, Pepper ¼oz, per man.

There shall also be allowed weekly, Vinegar not exceeding ¼ pint per man, for occasional use only when actually required, but not to be expended unnecessarily, nor considered as subject to be paid for when not used.

Suet and Raisins, or Suet and Currants, shall be substituted for ¼ part of the before-mentioned proportion of Flour, half of the said fourth part in Suet, and the other half in Raisins or Currants, at the following rates, viz: ½lb of Suet, or 1lb of Raisins, or ½lb of Currants, is to be considered equal to 1lb of Flour.

In case it should be found necessary to issue substitutes for any of the foregoing species of Provisions: ¼lb of Soft Bread, or 1lb of Rice, or 1lb Sago, or 1lb of Flour, is to be considered equal to 1lb of Biscuit.

½ pint of Wine, or 1 quart of Strong Beer, or ½ gallon of Small Beer, is to be considered equal to ½ gill of Spirits.

1oz of Coffee, 1oz of Cocoa, 1oz of Chocolate, ¼oz of Tea, are to be considered equal to each other.

1lb of Sago, 1lb of Scotch Barley, 1lb of Pearl Barley, 1lb of Rice, are to be considered equal to each other.

1lb of Rice, or 1 pint of Calavances, or 1 pint of Dholl, or ½ pint of Split Peas is to be considered equal to 1 pint of Peas.

1lb of Rice, is to be considered equal to 1 quart of Oatmeal.

¼lb of Onions, or ¼lb of Leeks, is to be considered equal to 1lb of other Vegetables.

One point of note is that the scale of provisions shows unequivocally that the spirit ration, even though reduced to half a gill per day, was no longer an alternative. It now formed part of official provisions, thereby reinforcing the principle introduced in 1844, that rum was the sailor's right wherever he might serve. Beer and wine were at best only substitutes. The transition was complete.

The Admiralty Circular appears to be a masterpiece of psychological drafting. By placing the halving of the rum allowance below the increase in the meat and sugar rations, Their Lordships were reversing the order given by the Grog Committee; surely no accident.

It is also interesting to reflect that in its two hundred years of association with the Royal Navy, the quantity of rum issued daily had been reduced by three quarters in a brief span of only thirty years. Rum indeed ruled but had certainly passed its climacteric.

Model of the paddle frigate Gorgon whose name spelt backwards bore an electric message!

Now the grog, boys, the grog, boys,
bring hither
And fill, fill up true to the brim
May the mem'ry of Nelson ne'er wither
Nor the star of his glory grow dim

May the French from the English
ne'er sever
But both to their colours prove true
This Russian bear they must
thrash now or never
So three cheers for the Red, White and Blue

CHAPTER FIVE

The halycon years of grog

1850 - 1918

I T WAS ALL VERY WELL for the country to indulge in patriotic songs with such words as the verse of *Britannia the Pride of the Ocean,* but in the early 1850's, the navy was in no fit state to indulge in sabre-rattling, or to engage in the full-blown war which Crimea was to become. The French, as so often in the past, had shown a lead in ship design coupled now with a willingness to experiment with steam, and they had advanced their gunnery by inventing the explosive shell, shortly to revolutionise warship construction. From the Royal Navy's point of view, it was a blessing that the Crimean conflict was mainly military with the French as its ally, almost as though Nelson had never existed. Most senior officers, apart from being far too old to lead fleets into battle, showed an appalling rigidity of mind and an inability to face new problems. Exceptions were few but one was Rear Admiral Berkeley, the Second Sea Lord at this time, who had been a member of the 1850 Grog Committee as can be seen from his signature at the foot of the Admiralty Circular reproduced on page 79.

The circular is full of a circumlocution typical of the age, but its numerous provisions are enlightening. While the recasting of seamen's pay at a daily rate, for example, may seem an insignificant administrative change, it was a revolutionary step of great benefit to the Victorian sailor. The halving of the grog ration undoubtedly must have been unpopular, but the compensatory money grant for those who did not wish to take grog at all, encouraged the men to become more temperate in their habits. These and other benefits were due to the reforming zeal of Admiral Berkeley who achieved even greater distinction by piloting the first Continuous Service Act through the Admiralty. The Order in Council embodying the Act was issued on April 1, 1853 to 'catch them young' for service in the Royal Navy. On attaining the age of eighteen, boy entrants were to be liable for ten years continuous service. There was to be greater concentration on preliminary training together with extra pay, pensions after twenty years' service, a new rate of leading seaman, and so on — all additional attractions for those wishing to make the navy their career.

The changes were profound. Previously manning had been hand-to-mouth, amounting to little more than bondage. Now, with long serving volunteers, the navy could regard itself more legitimately as a permanent arm of the country's defences, a standing force of professionals trained and attuned to demands of peace or war. The Continuous Service Act set the pattern for other far-reaching reforms later in the decade. By 1860, the navy was cast in the mould that broadly serves it today.

When rum was consolidated in the daily scale of provisions, it acquired an unaccustomed respectability, like that of the reluctant swain whose long engagement precedes eventual marriage. Rum's relationship before betrothal had been emotional and disturbed, but stability lay ahead. There were dissenters at the wedding who, while having 'no cause or just impediment why these two should not be joined together', could still lament, as did one seaman, that 'everything gets worse and worse . . . when we first went to sea, we used to have our quart of grog a day; now they serve out tea. It may do all very well in peace but it won't do in war. Only let them Yankees get hold of you, they'll l'arn you it.'

As for the navy in general, it could not be said that it had yet broken away completely from Winston Churchill's generalisation of its traditions as those of 'rum, sodomy and the lash'. But enlightenment was approaching, and the year 1850 probably represents that turning point when to the Victorian, the navy of Nelson and Collingwood appeared prehistoric. For example, take the provision in the Admiralty Circular of 1850 which withdrew or reduced rum privileges for seamen boys depending on their age: is it possible that the naval society of a hundred years before, would have been capable of such wise discrimination? Surely not.

The reduction of the daily rum ration to one eighth of a pint heightened the need to substitute quality for quantity. The victualling board's duty, now that rum formed part of the seaman's official ration, was to make it yet more acceptable to him. Taste was important, but even bouquet began to play a part, much in the same way as it did — and does — with old cognac. Smell, after all, is a primary sense, and naval rum, no less than any other form of alcohol which has aged, entitled compulsive sniffers to have some influence on bouquet. The process of blending, therefore, accelerated from this time on until an established blend, primarily of Demerara and Trinidad rums, along with a small portion of other rums was finalised. The precise formula was always a closely guarded secret, and there is scant reference to it. Above all the rum broker had his own particular reason for keeping it quiet.

Here is a story of recent times by Mr P. Curtis, formerly a chief petty officer, to show just how important blending and taste have always been, 'One invasion during the 1939-45 war which has never been sufficiently reported was the invasion of "foreign" rums from such places as Australia and South Africa. These foreign varieties were rejected by the older members of the ship's company. As a dedicated tot drinker, and in my capacity as "chief pusser", I did my best to satisfy my shipmates, by mixing pukka and foreign, but nothing compared with the original pusser's to which we were accustomed.

'After the war, we still held large stocks of the foreign blends, particularly at Singapore where I happened to be, and so Their Lordships, in their infinite wisdom, decided that the superintending victualling store officer should ascertain the exact blend of rum most acceptable to the post-war navy.

'In *HMS Terror*, the shore base in Singapore, there were no less than six chief pussers serving at the same time. The SVSO had a brainwave — who better than those six to give an impartial but balanced judgement?

'Consequently the six of us mustered in his office, furnished with a large table, chairs, samples of rum from everywhere, with cheese, butter, dry biscuits, etc, for cleaning the palate after each sip. The normal method of judging wine is fourfold — the colour, the aroma or nose, the taste, and the aftertaste. Rum is different! As all old timers will know, the only way to drink a tot is to swallow it whole, grimace, and then sit down to appreciate the glow which spreads from the stomach and engenders that wonderful feeling of peace and general bonhomie.

'The tasting committee proceeded with its task — probably the most enjoyable two hours work that anyone could devise! After a short period for recovery, we dutifully sat down that evening and with a due sense of dedication collated our views. The outcome, as I remember it, was fifty-five percent Demerara, thirty percent Trinidad, with the remainder being rum from Natal and Mauritius. My memory of that blend remains undimmed.'

For a final word on blending, in 1886, when an official investigation into rum losses took place at Deptford, a surveyor of the Board of Customs was invited to inspect the arrangements for stowing, vatting, reducing and issuing rum to the fleet. He commented, 'The most notable part of the system pursued consists in the blending and transfer of the rum from vat to vat, and I am of the opinion that it is admirably designed to improve the quality of the liquor.'

Is it possible that even he was under constraint not to provide detail on the blending in a report which would be available for many eyes to read?

Of lesser consequence than rum's flavour, but still important, was the colour. When distilled, rum is as colourless as gin — or water! Therefore it was necessary to give rum colour before supply to ships and, fortuitously, seamen also favoured a dark colour. The addition of caramel or dark sugar to the rum provided the required answer both to satisfy officialdom and personal preference.

The responsibility for receiving, stowing and issuing rum aboard ship devolved upon that much disliked man, the purser. His unpopularity stemmed from a system which permitted him only a small salary for being what was, in effect, the ship's business manager. His appointment by an Admiralty warrant tacitly acknowledged that his main remuneration would be through commissions on the items he purveyed, and the 'purser's pound' of fourteen instead of sixteen ounces was not something of his own invention, but an abuse openly allowed by authority. He could make a good thing out of his job only by indulging in what to others seemed to be downright peculation, and the list of abuses are too long to mention. The expression Pusser's Tricks became a by-word in the navy.

Nevertheless, as the nineteenth century progressed, the

majority of pursers were found to be honest, hardworking, and dedicated to providing the best for ships' companies. Their status improved when they were made responsible for disbursing small amounts of money to the men. In 1851, almost in step with the changes brought about by the Grog Committee, the purser's anomalous position was corrected. On assuming the title of Paymaster in that year, he shed most of the hostility which had attended his previous title. He was given a proper salary and allotted the task of paying all wages; needless to say, those extras which had been his earlier right, were abolished. As head of a ship's department and of wardroom rank, the new Paymaster rapidly became a respected person in the ship's hierarchy. His improved standing enabled him to maintain a beneficial relationship with the victualling board, and the victualling yards and created a harmony which was much to the advantage of the ship's company. He was, in a sense, the victualling board's representative afloat who could relay back to headquarters the likes and dislikes of a ship, and be the superviser of victualling trials whenever something new was introduced.

Fledgling officers, the midshipmen and mates, lived in an area known as the gunroom. They ranged in ages from twelve to twenty or older, a strange amalgam of the young and up-and-coming with those of more mature years whose promotion prospects were less rosy. They were divided informally into 'oldsters' and 'youngsters' and lived under a strange code of laws frequently involving strong-arm methods. The oldsters were permitted their daily allowance of rum of one eighth of a pint, but the younger element — or cadets as they were known — received none. A long established rule required the youngsters to leave the mess when two bells were sounded (9 pm) so that the oldsters could pursue their drinking. The moment was signalled by the senior member sticking a fork into the beam above his head, and summary punishment awaited those slow to withdraw. The fork-in-the-beam tradition spilled over into recent times, and the author remembers to his cost retribution in a battleship's gunroom between the world wars. There the similarity ended, for grog had long since been replaced by sherry or beer for the 'young gentlemen' (at their own expense by then).

The newly joined and credulous were always fair game for older members of the mess who never missed an opportunity to

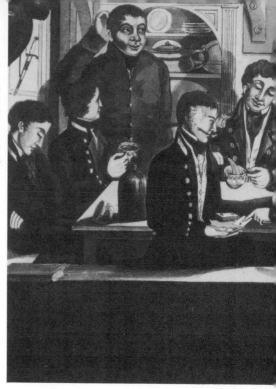

A midshipmen's mess (or gunroom) of 1821, the natural stepping stone to the wardroom for those who attained commissioned rank. From a naval officer's drawing

pull their legs when the chance offered. Admiral Dundas in his memoirs provides an account of his own experience after joining the gunroom of the *Thalia* on the China station as a sixteen-year-old midshipman, 'One day soon after I joined, the navigating midshipman said to me, "Look here, youngster, have you ever seen the rum served out?"

"No," I replied.

"Well, I am going ashore, and you must attend in my place."

"What have I to do?" I asked.

"Oh, you just go down to the steerage and stand alongside the ship's steward. When he says, "All ready, sir", you say, "Carry on, steward". Then you watch the different cooks of the messes come up and get their allowance of rum when the steward calls their names out. When he calls out "Gunroom three gills", you say "No steward, gunroom six gills", and that is all you have to do.

'I replied that I thought I could do that all right.

'It all went off very well; but I couldn't quite understand what they were all smiling at when I corrected the "stupid" mistake of

the ship's steward about the gunroom allowance.'

The gunroom had a regular visitor in the person of the school-master who was looked upon almost as an honorary member. Schoolie, a much-loved but sometimes eccentric character, came into his own in the mid-Victorian navy to provide a basic educa-tion for both officers and young seamen alike. By 1860, most schoolmasters were university graduates and of wardroom status. They taught their protegés in the gunroom, but some-times found it difficult to discipline their lively and unruly subjects. Admiral Dundas illustrated the point, 'Another cause of unrest was the issue of rum. All officers over eighteen years of age were allowed their tot as well as the men and this was served to them neat at eleven o'clock. The consequence was that when six bells struck all the senior midshipmen vanished like smoke and returned five minutes later smelling strongly of the West Indies spirit. This didn't help the naval instructor much.'

There is evidence to show that not only the *Thalia,* but many other ships served the grog ration at six bells (eleven o'clock) instead of the customary noonday issue of later years. An empty stomach filled with fiery liquid at eleven o'clock in the morning did no-one any good. It was the cause, not infrequently, of liver and stomach disease, and was superseded by the midday issue to enable Jack to lay a solid foundation of food before he began to lubricate.

Slowly the Admiralty came to realise that whatever could be done to improve the morale and character of men afloat must benefit the service. Education's advance manifested itself in more ways than one: the appointment of schoolmasters with university degrees was backed up, for example, by the creation of ships' libraries, a step which caused biographer John Bechervaise to wax lyrical, 'The establishment of libraries in the Royal Navy has more powerfully tended to improve the minds of seamen than can be supposed. For many years that I served as a petty officer before libraries were given, a book of any kind on a ship's lower deck was a grear rarity; and in any of the messes that had one, it was read and re-read and lent from man to man, until it became difficult to tell the original colour; and even these were of a kind that frequently injured rather than improved the morals of men. . . . How different it is now; everyone can get a book and read for himself. He can go to the library, take out a volume from a well-selected stock of books, and one day with another at sea, can have three hours to read and improve his mind.'

Such refinements, however, did not apply to those fighting the Crimean War which, in early 1856, was coming to an end. The British seaman had few opportunities to show his prowess in maritime conflict at this time, but ashore had performed outstandingly in support of the army. The formation in the 1840s of naval brigades for fighting ashore gained such impetus that, in the ensuing thirty years, they were required to serve in China and New Zealand (both for a second time), in Burma and Japan, and in Africa during the Ashantee and Zulu wars, and sometimes far inland during the Indian mutiny and in the short Abyssinian war.

The Crimea provided the opportunity for the Naval Brigade to distinguish itself. Led by their own officers, the men seemed to take particular delight in dealing with each new situation as though it were part of their normal life afloat; and, of course, they liked to impress the soldiers who thought them eccentric. Almost concurrently with the signing of the armistice, Queen Victoria introduced her own medal — the Victoria Cross — for which twenty-four naval officers and ratings, and two members of the Royal Marine Artillery, qualified retrospectively. The majority had served in the Naval Brigade under Admiral Keppel who, after taking command in 1855, wrote, 'They find our Jacks queer fellows; they deal in horses or anything else, and as soon as they come out of the trenches they are all over the soldiers' camps, doing work for the officers, repairing tents and that sort of thing, receiving part payment in grog and then share it with the first "sogger" they meet.'

In fact during the terrible sub-zero temperatures of the Crimean winter, the soldiers themselves were issued with a ration of rum each morning and evening. In the words of a sergeant-major of Dragoon Guards, 'Everyone admitted that it was the very best thing that the Commissariat ever did for the troops and it was duly appreciated.'

In these combined operations the seamen continued to receive his daily ration of grog whenever available; and the soldier was rewarded similarly during campaigns or on arduous duty, but his was not a daily issue as in the navy. But he was allowed an issue if he took passage in a warship whereupon he became 'entitled' during the embarked period. Jack, of course, was ever ready to take advantage if his soldier friend was slow to learn the ropes.

A case in point occurred this century in *HMS Albion* en route to Brunei with troops of the 1st King's Own Yorkshire Light Infantry. One particular day, writes Mr P A Childe of Sheffield, 'up spirits' was piped but one of the troops' messes failed to collect its ration. The corporal of the mess was piped for and asked why he had not collected the ration for his mess.

'We don't want any, sir. We've still got some from yesterday's issue,' he replied! Many were those who listened in silent disbelief, but on the following day numerous rum rats were seen in the vicinity of that mess around tot time!

There were many more far-sweeping changes towards the end of the Crimean conflict, some of which were later to affect the rum ration. One was the combined British-French naval bombardment of Kinburn pinpointing that historic moment when wooden sailing ships gave way to iron and steam. For the first time the sizeable force which took part was comprised wholly of steam vessels and achieved total success against the strongly-defended Russian fortifications. Additionally, there were three French armoured floating batteries which proved conclusively the value of armour. Admiralty found it salutary; had it been less conservative it could have had a fleet of fast screw ships with well-protected machinery from the outset of this protracted and expensive war. If armour had been employed the war might have ended earlier with an all-out attack from the sea on Russia's vulnerable Baltic ports. The consequence was that the ironclads soon to come into service would provide much improved stowage for that important commodity — rum.

A penalty of the long war was the manning problems it created, in turn highlighting the need to improve recruitment. The 1852 committee in introducing continuous service gave the sailor a guaranteed career, although its provisions were too limited. Consequently, in 1858 a Royal Commission was given the task of making further recommendations. Its report marked a turning point in the navy's social history by improving pensions and pay, instituting a reserve force, increasing length of service (which remained 'continuous'), and much else.

At this time the consumption of alcohol was mounting steadily throughout the country and affecting all classes of society. Understandably the daily rum ration did not escape the Commission's gaze. It was impracticable to reduce the ration further. There were only two choices — abolish it, hardly politic,

or increase the money allowance of those who elected to forego their daily grog.

They chose the latter.

Almost concurrently with the Commission's report, a standard uniform was introduced. With hindsight it seems unbelievable that such a decision should have taken so long. The deciding factor, of course, was the recently introduced long service engagement which brought the seaman more into line with the officer, who had had a recognisable uniform since 1748. The bluejacket resplendent in his new items of clothing, was taken into the hearts of the British public and his image popularised in song and dance.

There was a flaw in Jack's character, however; never a dull character ashore, he was too easily lured by the local tavern. There was need for him to change his ways partly — if not wholly — towards a philosophy of the three 't's — tea, temperance and teetotalism. There were those ready to help him steer a course in this direction, most notably Agnes Weston who devoted her life to supporting the moral welfare of seamen. Eldest daughter of a

The Anglo-French bombardment of Kinburn in the Black Sea. For the first time all the warships taking part were powered by steam

successful barrister, she was indefatigable in encouraging the building of sailors' homes in the naval ports with all attendant comforts bar alcohol. A byword in the Royal Navy for a hundred years or more, 'Aggie' was used familiarly by all; even a warship named after Weston-super-Mare was commonly called by the sailor 'Aggie-on-Horseback'.

In 1866 the strength of the rum issue was prescribed as 4.5 under proof, at which level it remained thereafter. All rum came from the West Indies and was bought from samples lying in bond at the docks. It was then transferred to Deptford where it was started in vats varying in capacity from 4,000 gallons to upwards of 32,000 gallons. Demerara from what was then British Guiana, now Guyana, constituted the bulk of the liquid, with Trinidad rum added for lightness, and a small percentage from Barbados, Cuba, Martinique and elsewhere. Samples of the various blends were kept by technical experts, and tasting panels were convened whenever there were complaints or major changes in bulk supply. The process had become so sophisticated not to say scientific, that costs could be kept down by using cheaper rums in the blend without losing the all important and special flavour that came to be the hallmark of Admiralty rum.

On one occasion it became necessary to examine one of the largest vats to explode a popular myth that a missing pet dog had fallen in. Upon emptying it no skeleton was found, only a variety of bottles with strings attached, which were believed to have been let down by a thirsty and ingenious member of the work-force who cast all asunder when detection loomed. Nevertheless, there were occasional discoveries of snakes, frogs and other creatures in the huge puncheons transporting the rum, and that constant companion of mess life onboard — the cockroach — frequently became rum-preserved.

Rum was sometimes found to be below issuing proof, and sailors reacted immediately. Queen's Regulations and Admiralty Instructions of the 1870 period introduced a meticulous scale for adding more rum and keeping back an equal quantity of water when mixing grog in order to bring it up to strength. Vernon's ghost ever lurked in the shadows at the merest hint of men being 'defrauded' of their allowance!

With Britain deeply engaged in social improvements and evangelical zeal, the mid-victorian navy was an obvious target for reformers. But such reform was by no means the prerogative of well-meaning civilians. Miss Agnes Weston's untiring efforts to improve the quality of seamen's lives ashore were equalled by Admiralty's endeavours to humanise discipline afloat. Punishment varied, from the imposition of six-water grog, at one extreme, to imprisonment with hard labour and dismissal from the service at the other, but the incidence of flogging in the fleet fell rapidly.

Rum, alas, could still be the root cause of misdemeanour, although responsible for only a proportion of drinking offences.

Provision was made for its stowage in the ironclads now coming into service with their well ventilated spaces set aside for spirit rooms. The design drawings of the first armoured battleship, the *Warrior* completed in 1860, a match for all her existing line-of-battle consorts put together, show her to have had such a room. Entry was by hatch from the lower deck just abaft the mainmast into a sizeable compartment, another 'first' among the many attributed to this outstanding ship. But it is equally evident from the Returns of Courts Martial, that in older and smaller ships with less secure stowage, temptation could arise as these examples from the 1867 returns illustrate,

'John Picton, carpenter's crew, *HMS Adventure.*
First charge — Drunk onboard ship.
Second charge — Having concealed on his person a bottle belonging to the Crown, containing a portion of rum which appeared to have been stolen from a cask in the baggage room by the forcing of a bulkhead.
First proved. Second proved except that there was no evidence that he had any knowledge or connection with the theft of the rum. Adjudged to be reduced to the second class for conduct and punished with forty-eight lashes.
'Joseph Williams, steward third class, *HMS Rosario.*
First charge — Hiding away a cask of rum, the property of the Crown, and stealing a portion of its contents.
Second charge — Drunk onboard ship.
Both charges proved. Disrated, reduced to the second class for conduct, imprisoned for one year with hard labour and dismissed from HM Service.
'James Smith, private RM, *HMS Barracouta.*
First charge — Obtaining keys of after hold and broaching a cask of spirits.

Second charge — Accidentally or otherwise setting fire to the said spirits, leaving the spot without giving information, thereby greatly endangering the ship.
Both charges proved. Imprisoned for one year with hard labour and dismissed from HM Service.'

John Picton was unlucky to be given forty-eight lashes, for in 1871, just four years later, the Admiralty issued an instruction suspending all corporal punishment in peacetime. He may well have had the unenviable distinction of being the last recorded example of that unhappy relationship between rum and lash.

In the mid 1860's, The Admiralty instituted an enquiry into all aspects of discipline and punishment and invited the views of most flag officers and captains-in-command. The edited replies were circulated widely which was a good way of stimulating and encouraging further thought. In this report appeared the first pleas for the total abolition of rum, with suggestions for substituting beer and wine when practicable. One proposal was that a pint of beer should be allowed to those who elected to spend their evening leave aboard. The intention, of course, was to restrict the run ashore which, more often than not, resembled a Bacchanalian orgy. Few seamen, however, went along with the view of some of their number who told the Royal Naval Temperance Society that they wished for 'a public house without the drink'. Attitudes were certainly changing in the minds of naval men but the pace could not be forced. Statistics, however, show that it was not until 1876 that the per capita consumption of alcohol in the United Kingdom reached its highest point. The contest between grog and temperance was to go the full fifteen rounds.

While temperance was urged upon the lower deck, an equal need for its observance existed in the wardroom. The quantities of duty-free wines and spirits permitted to admirals and other officers were far too generous, even allowing for increasing official entertaining. It is difficult to follow the reasoning behind the retention of the rum ration for officers and if the 1850 Grog Committee erred in any way, it was surely in this regard. Perhaps they felt that as rum henceforward was to be included in the daily scale of provisions, then officers had an equal entitlement.

In the early 1860's drunkenness was as much a social evil

among officers as it was on the lower deck — perhaps more so as they had greater opportunity for drinking in private. Attacks of *delirium tremens* were not uncommon and although these were self-inflicted, those concerned escaped with invaliding or were allowed to resign. Their Lordships slowly came to realise that behaviour which was 'to the prejudice of good order and naval discipline' should be treated as such and an Admiralty letter dated May 4, 1863, ordered captains to court-martial officers for offences of drunkenness within this category, even providing a specimen charge to emphasise the point.

Issued by the RN branch, National Temperance League 1868

Their Lordships' strictures appear to have had the desired effect. The court martial returns for a typical half year from July to December, 1866, show that eighteen out of a total of twenty-six courts martial within this period were for drunkenness and associated offences — a far higher proportion than the returns show for similar offences on the lower deck. Notwithstanding, officers continued to receive their daily rum ration.

It was not until 1881 that the privilege was withdrawn but even then warrant officers were excepted and retained their rum ration until as late as 1918. This may seem anachronistic but social divisions then were much stronger. After all, warrant officers' roots were on the lower deck and rum was their birth-right to a greater extent than of the commissioned officer. Thankfully, such distinctions are now historic.

The 1850 Grog Committee had made a brave attempt to deny rum to adolescents by differentiating between midshipmen and cadets, and between seamen boys of the first and second classes. Only midshipmen and boys first-class were allowed the ration after 1850, and this at the captain's discretion. The committee would have done better — so hindsight suggests — by insisting on an age qualification instead of passing the buck to captains whose views on entitlement varied considerably. Apart from the moral aspect of whether it was good for a youngster of seventeen or eighteen to drink spirits, the daily issue also interfered with his training as already discussed. But from 1881 — along with other officers — his tot was a thing of the past. At the same time the opportunity was seized to raise the qualifying age for seamen to draw their rum to twenty. Those affected received the usual monetary compensation until 1930 when it was decided that if a man was under age for rum he was equally unentitled to grog money. History makes administrators wise!

While these changes were taking place in the 1880's the temperance societies were in full cry through the medium of demonstrations, public speakers, periodicals, journals and sponsored pamphlets. From 1890, the sailor's shoregoing leave had ceased to be a privilege; provided he was of good character, and the exigencies of the service allowed, he could now take leave regularly as a right. The bluejacket in his distinctive uniform bcame a familiar sight in most urban surroundings and a target for the reformers.

The navy's rum was heavily under fire, but while many suggestions for reform were made with good intentions, others seemed to be laced heavily with Victorian prudery. A leading article by 'Publicist' in the *Naval and Military Record* of March 9, 1899, had this to say,

'Suggestions for reform

The grog allowance in the navy is an absurd and injurious anachronism. It is not necessary that one should be a total abstainer to concur in this statement. What would be said of a private employer who engaged men and paid them a certain wage and a daily tot of spirit? In the case of an individual employer such a contract would be illegal. It would be contrary to the provisions of the Truck Act, and would be justly denounced. The Admiralty pose as model employers not only in the dock-yards, but in the fleet. The custom of giving to each man a tot of rum every day has survived for so many years that numerous abuses have sprung up which should be put down with a firm hand. While many reformers object to the granting of the grog allowance under any circumstances, most persons would be quite satisfied if men were really free to take it or leave it.'

After this somewhat muddled thinking, and a long account of

the opinions of a number of officers, 'Publicist' continued, 'The question, however, may be raised whether the time has not arrived when the grog allowance of the navy should be put on a less injurious basis. It is impossible to justify regulations which practically force men to incur the opprobrium of their fellows, or to commit an offence against their own consciences or against the Queen's regulations. Let it be clearly understood the sudden suspension of the grog allowance is not advocated. By a large section of the men it is appreciated, and its withdrawal would cause discontent, and probably do incalculable harm. If, however, the Admiralty could see their way to a simplification of the methods by which men at present obtain a monetary equivalent instead of drink they would do all that could be reasonably expected. The allowance at present amounts only to about 4s 4d a quarter. If the authorities could see their way to give a penny a day to every man who elected not to take up his daily tot they would inaugurate a reform which would be welcomed by the better class of men of the navy, and by the general public, who always take an affectionate interest in all that affects the best interest of the men of the fleet. If the belief is well-founded that a very large number of men would abandon the daily ration of drink and accept payment in lieu thereof, the additional money thus spent would be well laid out.'

Platitudes and non-sequiturs follow to the article's bitter end. Yet in proposing a monetary daily allowance to replace the small monthly savings allowance introduced by the 1850 Grog Committee, the writer was on the right lines. But he had stirred a hornet's nest as these extracts from 'Nauta' and 'Nemo' in the following week's edition of the *Naval and Military Record* show: 'Rum having superseded beer, and grog having superseded rum, it will be seen that for centuries alcohol has been recognised as an article of diet in the navy. When the question arises as to whether it is advisable to abolish the grog ration several complex problems spring at once to the mind of the inquirer, but before any reform is instituted the whole question of victualling must be examined. A seaman or stoker cannot be compared with a dockyard or shore employee; the ship is his workshop and his home. His work, his food, his bed, and his beverages are comprised within the stem and the stern of the ship. At sea he cannot go to his pub or his club for a drink. Let it be granted that the rum ration is an evil, what is to be put in its place? The man who can solve this problem will answer a question that has not only puzzled admirals and captains, but he will solve the whole temperance question.' *Nauta*

'The seamen of the fleet are not paid a certain wage and a daily tot of spirits. They are paid a certain wage and a certain daily allowance of provisions, which includes amongst other items tea, sugar, rum etc, and it is in my opinion much to be deplored that in articles of the description written by *Publicist* capital should be attempted to be made out of one item of that allowance of provisions, as viewed from a temperance standpoint, and based upon a very imperfect knowledge of the facts involved.' *Nemo*

Nemo had diagnosed the complaint without providing the cure while *Publicist* had obliged with the cure without knowledge of the symptoms. The age-old problem was the Savings System by which ships' messes not taking up their full daily allowance could use the value of their savings to buy other items of their choice. Those who chose not to draw their rum ration received an inadequate monthly compensation. Up to a point it was the system which militated against temperance. If the Admiralty wished to encourage fewer men to take their grog, then proper compensation with a daily cash allowance was one way of accomplishing it. A useful by-product could well be a lessening in the trading and trafficking of rum.

The plunge was taken and the Admiralty decided to introduce an allowance of one half-penny a day which has no ring of generosity, but at least it was an improved and positive form of compensation.

A few years later, in 1907, the allowance was discussed again when the Victualling Votes were before Parliament. Referring to the rum ration, the Secretary to the Navy, Mr E Robertson, said that, 'Temperance men are labelled 'T' in ships' books. At present twenty-five per cent of them are so marked and yearly there is an increase of one per cent. As an inducement to teetotalism it was proposed to raise the allowance from nine-sixteenth's of a penny a day to one penny, costing on present numbers £22,000 as against £7,000 annually. It was also proposed that men taking the grog allowance should be labelled in the books 'G'. Mr Leif Jones expressed peculiar satisfaction with the statement of the Secretary to the Navy. He considered the cost would be no more than £15,000 a year on present numbers and he urged that an enormous advantage would be gained to the efficiency of the navy by the total abolition of the rum ration.'

The allowance was duly raised to a penny, as proposed, and finally in 1919 to threepence a day.

A statistical return in 1913 for ships of the Channel fleet, including the Royal Naval barracks at Portsmouth, Devonport and Chatham, provides some interesting detail,

	Numbers victualled	Elected draw spirit	Elected to receive money allowance
June 30, 1913	30,797	19,703	3,363
December 1, 1913	33,297	21,774	3,772

Of the numbers entitled to exercise an option, 14.58% preferred the money allowance in June, and 14.76% in December, which compares unfavourably with the twenty-five percent of a few years earlier. Too much should not be read into this as the trend towards abstention continued. The figures do reveal a large under-age percentage who were therefore unentitled. Admiral Lord Charles Beresford was able to reflect in his memoirs that 'sobriety is, happily, the fashion now (1914).'

The lower deck possessed a friend and advocate in Admiral Sir John Fisher throughout those formative years of the early twentieth century. He is probably better known for his untiring efforts to update the *materiel* of the fleet and for his great brainchild — the *Dreadnought* — which took a bare six months to build from first laying down her keel to her launching in Portsmouth dockyard. Of equal importance however were his measures to improve the conditions of service for seamen while Second Sea Lord and responsible for personnel and training. Notably, he transferred training from unhealthy and cramped hulks afloat to new and spacious barracks ashore at the three major naval ports. His concern for the welfare of the men knew no bounds and by them he was always affectionately referred to by them as 'Jackie' Fisher, the seaman's friend. But 'Jackie' did not interfere with the rum ration. He simply created the civilised life around it which encouraged the average seaman to treat his long-standing privilege with respect and some decorum.

Rum indeed compensated in part for the hardships and privations of World War I, no less for the soldier than the sailor as it turned out. Probably the severest ordeal the soldier had to bear was the prolonged deprivation and discomfort of trench warfare and many of those with memories of the bitter winters spent in the trenches have endorsed the value of a generous, but carefully controlled rum issue. So it was for the sailor in his own environment, but the days were approaching when, for quite different reasons, the daily rum ration was to come under fire again.

At ten to twelve each forenoon
Since the Navy first began
Jack drinks the health of Nelson
From Jutland to Japan

He's always done his duty
To country and the throne
And all he asks in fairness
Is leave his tot alone

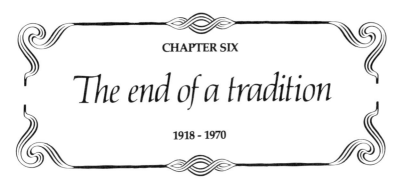

THE SPREAD OF EDUCATION, and the provision of rival interests to the public house, caused a dramatic change in social habits towards the end of the nineteenth century. There was an increasing interest in sport and outdoor life in general, and the growth of clubs also helped to encourage a more temperate society. Against this background the many temperance movements which existed in Britain were achieving remarkable success. In particular the Royal Army Temperance Association and the Royal Naval Temperance Society helped encourage a decent and sober way of life. As a result, both the spiral of consumption of alcohol and the prevalence of drunkenness continued downwards steeply between 1900 and 1918, but attempts by moralists to interfere with the navy's daily rum ration met fierce resistance.

Nor was Admiralty at this time in any mood to meddle with the ration. The board knew from long experience that, for many individuals the importance of rum out-ran any other item of the daily provisions, and that even if they accepted the need for change, timing would be vital. Thus the reductions of 1824 and 1850 had been made when reaction was likely to be minimal, and by so planning the board had shown considerable wisdom. The early 1900's, with war clouds threatening yet again after the Boer War, was not the moment to countenance further concession to the temperance lobby. When the Great War did arrive the rum ration proved to be an invaluable comfort to those who chose to draw it — particularly since the bitter cold North Sea was the main scene of naval action, and restricted leave made it difficult for men to gain solace ashore. Even then the new pub laws dramatically restricted hours of business compared with the ever-open doors of earlier years.

Rum, too, helped to make monotonous wartime cooking more palatable. Dinner might not have been recognised by a *cordon bleu* cook but after a tot it seemed edible. The 'matelot's built-in stabiliser', as rum was sometimes called, had much in its favour and the numbers taking grog for 1914 support the argument that rum was undoubtedly popular. Of the total naval strength of 131,000 men, 88,200 were more than twenty years of age and therefore entitled. Some 77,000 (eighty-seven per cent) actually drew their daily rum.

With the inflated numbers of seamen required to man the fleets of two world wars, the logistic problems of supplying rum to ships and overseas bases were immense. Estimating annual purchases, bonding, vatting, blending, and distributing, demanded experience and foresight on the part of the victualling department. The fact that they were able to cope with as much as a sudden trebling of peacetime requirements, provides remarkable testimony to the department's efficiency which has largely passed unnoticed and unsung.

There were possibilities, too, of abnormal losses to upset calculations. As far back as 1886, when an enquiry into large shortfalls at Deptford took place, it was discovered that if the level of rum in a vat was allowed to fall below two feet, the rate of loss caused by evaporation rose dramatically. Then, too, a vat by the nature of its construction, could never be placed out of use even temporarily — as had sometimes happened — without considerable wastage.

Deptford experienced with misfortune on two occasions in this century, both so enormous in scale that again it is a tribute to the victualling department that they could carry on business without a break.

In the first of these disasters in 1927, the Thames flooded, and the waters invading the rum cellars ruined the entire stock, including the well-matured rum used for blending. In 1941, when heavy shipping losses jeopardised supplies, Deptford with its storage of more than a quarter of a million gallons of rum was a victim of the London blitz, the Royal Victoria Yard receiving much damage from fire and water.

The second world war provided its peculiar problems as, year by year, it became increasingly difficult to obtain rum from West

Indian sources. Demands to the broker had to take account of all those puncheons of overproof spirit which German submarines were committing to the seabed. At one stage, serious thought was given to the idea of supplying ships with rum of greater strength than that of the normal four point five underproof as one means of saving valuable shipping space, but it was thought it would have had serious complications and was not pursued. Things became so critical in 1943 that the Admiralty was forced seriously to consider discontinuing rum which, for reasons of morale, the board was loathe to do. A solution was found in the nick of time by the Treasury's agreement to buy expensive and immature rum from Cuba and Martinique to make up the million gallons that were needed each year. This was no straightforward deal as the stocks came from a non-Commonwealth source and had already been bespoken.

Rum from Natal was available in quantity for supply to ships in south east Asian and far eastern waters but, unblended, it was far from popular, particularly as 'taste' was rum's most important quality in hot climates. And taste was not Natal rum's strong point. A typical reaction is provided by an armed merchant cruiser which slid into Colombo harbour in 1943, and shortly afterwards lodged a demand which included twenty-five gallons of rum. However the lighter delivering the stores to the cruiser brought back all twenty-five gallons without explanation. A signal was sent to the ship requesting the reason for its return and for the normal report of survey. Nothing happened until the ship was passing the breakwater on the way to sea when she made, 'Your 1133. Report of survey is on the way to you. Rum returned as it is the only drink ever received which made us wish we were teetotallers. Place of origin Durban.'

The rum was pure Natal, produced by a distillery called the National Chemical Syndicate which supplied the Admiralty until 1961. Natal rum normally matured in oak casks for five years in Britain. There were, on average, three shipments per annum in puncheon casks each containing between ninety and one hundred and ten imperial gallons. Until 1956, shipments were made to Alexandria, but thereafter supplies went only to London.

It was not only at sea that losses occurred. Shore bases maintaining stocks of rum could be overrun, as nearly happened when Rommel threatened Alexandria in 1942. *HMS Boston*, almost the last ship in harbour, had the task of destroying casks left behind when Egyptian storemen evacuated the base. The contents of these casks and jars could be decided by the colour of the bands or marks upon them — red for rum, green for limejuice, and white for vinegar, but all were axed without discrimination, painful for those seamen who had to perform the committal rites and typical of the problems facing the victualling department.

Again, before the fall of Hong Kong in December 1941, thousands of gallons of rum were poured into the sea to deny its use to the Japanese or more likely to the local Chinese who had acquired a taste for it.

The twenty-year interval between wars was a stable period in rum's history although there was one important change made, the last before its abolition as it turned out. It had been represented in a review of service conditions that grog would be more acceptable with less water in the mix, and trials were carried out in 1937 and implemented a year later. The puritan-minded viewed the change with disfavour, and in a way it did savour of putting the clock back. Strangely, the Admiralty had shown little concern about the quantity of water to be added to make grog as the early regulations (see chapter two), referring simply to adding 'a due proportion of water' or, 'the usual proportion' clearly show. When the results of the trial showed that a change to two-water grog (two parts of water to one of rum), would be infinitely preferred to the existing three-water grog, and that the trial itself had been carried out without adverse consequence, Their Lordships were prepared to consider the matter. A Select Committee consisting of the Fourth Sea Lord (responsible for supplies), the Director of Victualling and other celebrities, tasted samples of the various mixtures laid before them and approved the change to two-water grog. The unexplained disappearance of the left-overs from this experiment obviously had a connection with the behaviour of some of the Admiralty messengers later that day. In many ways two-water grog would have been more convenient administratively in wartime, with the added benefit of retaining its flavour and quality for a longer period, although there is nothing to suggest that the Admiralty approved the change with such thoughts in mind.

In the submarine service the custom developed of mixing grog in equal quantities of rum and water (one for one), for which, so far as is known, no regulation provided. Submariners have ever shown a sturdy independence; the grog mix would have been regarded as within the province of individual commanding officers to rule.

Towards the end of the second world war Britain had amassed a sizeable Pacific fleet to support her American ally in the final assault of Japan. The essential task for the British navy was the reduction of bases in the Sakishima Gunto group of islands which lie to the east of Taiwan. Except for the aircrews involved in direct combat, the bulk of ships' companies found it a relatively dull existence. The monotony of long hours of immediate readiness and stand-by in a humid and enervating climate was relieved only occasionally by a Japanese Kamikazi pilot breaking cloud overhead. There were few opportunities for rest or leisure to interrupt the long periods at sea, and then it was only to repair to a large anchorage such as Leyte Gulf in the Philippines where shore leave was impossible. However, such temporary withdrawals from the scene of action provided the opportunity for a loving rendezvous with a fleet auxiliary from Sydney fully stocked with beer. Transfers of beer to ships and free issues to all were made with great despatch. The sight of the greater part of the ship's company of a fleet aircraft carrier contentedly downing bottles of strong Australian beer on the flightdeck is one which will ever live in the memory of those who saw it. In a thirst-creating climate, the lesson was learned again that to many beer was more acceptable than the daily issue of rum. For some time the Admiralty had been exploring ways of making it regularly available as can be seen from the historical note on beer in Appendix II.

That wartime experiment with a fleet auxiliary had a greater significance for to some extent beer was regaining its pre-eminence, not as a replacement for rum, but increasingly as a possible alternative in the peace which lay ahead. It was not long before beer was carried aboard ship for purchase by seamen at the rate of a can of beer per day.

As things turned out, the immediate post-war years provided little opportunity for dwelling on social reforms while the navy remained fully extended in a disturbed world. The release of conscripts left barely sufficient numbers to undertake the navy's many commitments, ranging from war situations like that in

Korea to assisting in the orderly withdrawals from a diminishing empire. All the same, in the mid 1950's Their Lordships found time to consider seriously the abolition of rum and its possible replacement with beer. The navy's strength by then was about 100,000 men of whom roughly 32,000 took their daily grog. This number was decreasing yearly and evidence presented by the naval commands pointed to the acceptance of beer as a substitute provided — and here was the rub — it could be stowed aboard. Admiral Lord Mountbatten, then First Sea Lord, was not himself a great rum lover but with foresight he realised the great change that was about to take place in ships and those who manned them. In a matter of years complex warships would enter service requiring crews trained to handle highly sophisticated equipment, for which the stalwart three-badge able seaman accustomed to his daily rum would be a misfit.

Unfortunately, the extra space required for stowing the large stocks of beer that ships would need to carry, could not be provided by the spirit room alone, and valuable ammunition spaces, which were available in peace but not in war, could not be sacrificed at the altar of beer. So undecided the matter stood although the conviction that there was really no place for rum in a modern navy became firmly rooted.

Before long, rum was the subject of public debate, because of rumour and counter-rumour over its future. With so much at stake for its readers, the daily press in the naval ports was probably the most vociferous. The *Portsmouth Evening News* kept track of developments from an early date as the following extracts show.

'April 16, 1960,—Stop navy rum ration in home ports.

'So said a representative at the national conference of the Order of Good Templars who believed that serious incidents at home ports were directly attributable to the rum ration. Reaction was quick as typified by Seaman James Reynolds of *HMS Victory*, "The Admiralty would never do it. I cannot imagine what would happen on the lower deck if they stopped our tots. It is time these temperance people kept their views to themselves. Nobody minds their not drinking so long as they do not try to ruin other people's pleasure." '

This was followed two days later on April 18 under the heading, Attacking the navy's rum, 'The evils of strong drink, which helped to create the Good Templars, are not quite what they were when the movement was founded, and men of the Royal Navy were surprised at the week-end to find their daily rum ration under attack. If true temperance is moderation, the issue of one-eighth of a pint might be regarded as being most abstemious, but if teetotallers lack practical experience, they make up for it with facts and figures. Crimes of all kinds, including murder, are blamed on the grog barrel.'

Then a year or two of relative silence until March 2, 1964, when a special article headed, Tottering tot of the navy, asks, 'Will sailors in the Royal Navy get their rum in plastic bags, or will the ancient privilege be abandoned before the rum barrel is replaced?'

The author provided his own answer with convincing logic, 'To bring this ancient naval custom to an end would need courage, but the fact that the suggestion is raised usually once a year, is evidence of the belief that the days of the tot are numbered. Of course there would be a "hue and cry" from the lower deck, but this old-age privilege is not held with such conviction or esteem as it was in the days of the old salt. . . .'

He continued, 'Of the 32,000 who are recorded as drawing their daily tot, a large proportion do so for the following reasons:

(a) That it is not worth their while not to because a tot of the same proof ashore (assuming you could get it) would be worth, duty paid, eight shillings . . . the mere psychological value of drawing it is obvious.

(b) Bravado. You might be called a cissie if you did not draw it.

(c) There is the chance of getting in favour with a senior rating by illegally giving him "sippers", or even, again illegally, by "flogging it".'

Rum was kept in the forefront of the public's mind by a series of articles over the next two or three years on the dying art of the cooper in the navy and other subjects allied to rum. There followed on October 23, 1967, an item headed 'Breathalyser does not halt grog'. The connection between drinking and driving as a cause of road accidents was now under heavy fire. The breathalyser had been introduced and the navy's daily rum was criticised on that account. A defensive Ministry said in this article, 'Experimental tests under police supervision at HMS Caledonia, Rosyth, showed two petty officers and a leading seaman were unfit to drive after drinking their daily rum ration. Though the three were perfectly sober, a signal has gone out to all shore establishments warning ships' companies to take care if they drive soon after taking their grog.'

On September 3, 1969, there were distinct straws in the wind under the heading, That's rum!, 'The navy's rum issue may now be stopped! Ministry of Defence chiefs are considering ways of compensating seamen for the loss of this old custom. A MOD spokesman said, "It is true we have given this matter consideration, but no decision has been taken on the timing, compensation or any alternative measures." '

Two months later, on November 12, 1969, the naval correspondent showed his ability as a press sleuth, Tot tottering as navy seeks compensation, 'The popular bosun's call Up Spirits — which for two centuries and more has brought sailors tumbling from their messes to the rum tub — may not be piped aboard the Queen's warships much longer. For the tot, as I reported in this column in September, is decidedly tottering.

'One form of replacement for the daily rum ration will be considered at an Admiralty meeting next week. Under consideration is a scheme whereby chief and petty officers will be able to buy a daily ration of duty-free spirits and the leading seamen and below will receive some compensation as part of the new military salary to be announced in the New Year.'

Then on December 18, 1969, came the farewell to the tot and with such expressions as 'the tourniquet is to be applied' and 'as predicted in *The News* last month', the naval correspondent with a flourish of self vindication finally broke the news of rum's abolition commenting, 'The decision should not come as a shock. Four years ago this newspaper advised the matelot "The days of the tot are numbered." '

The long alliance of rum and the Royal Navy had ended. That Admiralty was sensitive to all it meant, and had meant, to generations of seamen, is shown in their signal sent on December 17, 1969, 'The Admiralty Board have reviewed the daily issue of rum in the light of the conditions and needs of the modern navy.

2 Rum is a particular naval privilege of very long standing and one which is cherished and enjoyed. The Board has given full weight to this fact. It has, on the other hand, concluded that a daily issue of rum is no longer compatible with the high standards of efficiency required now that the tasks in ships are concerned with complex, and often delicate machinery and

systems, on the correct functioning of which people's lives may depend.

3 The Board decided that this conclusion is over-riding and that in the interests of safety and efficiency in the fleet the rum issue should be abolished provided that suitable compensating advantages could be arranged for the benefit of the fleet. Grog money at threepence a day, broadly represents the cost of the present issue to the Crown. It would not pay for a daily beer issue. Nor does it represent a significant daily payment to individuals.

4 By way of financial compensation a lump sum of £2.7 million will be paid into a new fund for the purpose of providing social and recreational facilities for the welfare of ratings and RM other ranks. The fund, which will be known as the Sailors' Fund, will have a substantial income. This will be used for charitable purposes to benefit past and present naval ratings and Royal Marines, other ranks and their dependents. Ratings will take a major part in the administration of the fund.

5 In addition chief petty officers, petty officers and senior non-commissioned officers will be permitted to buy duty-free spirits in their messes up to a normal maximum of one-eighth pint per man per day in HM ships abroad and in Category 1 and 2 ships at home. In Category 3 ships purchase will be permitted at duty paid prices. Junior ratings (and RM equivalents) will be allowed to purchase up to a maximum of three cans of beer per day. They will not be allowed to purchase spirits. The new rules for the purchase of alcoholic drinks will provide facilities that are reasonable in the exacting circumstances of naval service and work.

6 Accordingly, the daily rum issue and grog money will be abolished from Saturday, August 1, 1970. Detailed instructions for the setting up and running of the Sailors' Fund, for the sale of spirits in senior ratings' messes, for the sale of beer to junior ratings and for the disposal of existing stocks of rum will be issued shortly by DCI (RN).'

The signal reveals the thoroughness — and the fairness — with which the Admiralty Board had treated this emotive subject; it followed the established practice of all naval signals in being concise, explicit, and devoid of ambiguity. It could not provide more than a short abstract of all the weighty arguments which had influenced those in high places to reach their decision. Many were involved including Mr Denis Healey, Secretary of State for Defence, Doctor David Owen, Parliamentary Under Secretary of State for Defence (Navy), and Admirals Sir Michael Le Fanu and Sir Frank Twiss — the First and Second Sea Lords respectively — who had the more direct responsibility.

Admiral Twiss provided his reminiscences of that occasion:

'I think I am right in saying that the rum issue was troubling Their Lordships as long ago as the late twenties and was brought to the notice of the Board in the thirties.

'Thereafter, the war and the immediate post-war period was no time for grappling with rum, and matters remained unconsidered until the introduction of tinned beer made it possible to carry alcohol in sufficient quantity to meet the needs of a ship's company.

'By the late 1950's ships were carrying large quantities of tinned (or sometimes keg) beer and provision of this luxury became a regular feature of replenishment at sea or in harbour. In order to regulate the consumption sailors were rationed to one can at dinner, paid for by the recipient, but taken almost as a chaser to the rum issue. In chief and petty officers messes bars were established for the sale of beer and the quantity drunk in these places was not well regulated.

'Concurrent with this development came the complete change in technology which took the navy from its pre-war and wartime horse and buggy equipment to the much more sophisticated, expensive and tailored material resulting from electronics, jet propulsion, missiles and atomic power. In short naval skills had

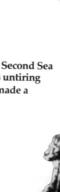

Admiral Sir Frank Twiss, Second Sea Lord in 1970. Through his untiring efforts the Sailors' Fund made a spirited start

changed from manpower, heavy equipment and self service to brain power, miniaturizing and go-no-go maintenance.

'During the 1960's social changes, notably in the relationship between officers and ratings, the introduction of entertainment in harbour by chief and petty officers' messes, improved standards of accommodation and the increasing take up of alcohol in the country as a whole began to give rise to serious anxiety to the flag officers of the three fleets (Home, Mediterranean and Far East). Evidence accumulated to indicate that some people were under the influence of alcohol while performing tasks on board where errors of judgement or manipulation could lead to death or major accidents to aircraft, ships or missiles, and practically every commanding officer of a ship commented in some form on the undesirable situation brought about by the issue of rum and the opportunity to purchase beer of a high alcoholic content. So much so that the three commanders-in-chief of the seagoing navy decided to raise the matter separately with the Board of Admiralty.

'In 1963/64 I was Flag Officer Flotillas Home Fleet and closely in touch with seagoing opinion and trends. In 1965, acutely aware of the drink problem in the navy, I went as Commander Far East Fleet where I soon had through my command a very high percentage of the fleet sent to combat the Indonesian confrontation crisis.

'In Singapore the problem of drink and the sailor became acute. Ships in harbour made the rum issue at noon and thereafter at weekends or in tropical routine men could proceed ashore, passing on their way to the dockyard gates a canteen where beer was on sale without limit. Frequently sailors owned or hired cars and the incidence of accidents attributable to drink became so serious that the commanding officer of the military hospital wrote to say that something had to be done to reduce the load on his hospital caused by car accidents.

'By this time I was convinced that the time had come to stop the free issue of rum. It was now completely inappropriate and outdated. What was suitable for sailing ships, heavy work in bad weather or geared to a life of physical effort, was quite out of keeping with a modern navy of air-conditioning, stabilizers, delicate electronic devices and the opportunity to obtain beer onboard. Accordingly I started some research to try and establish a factual measure of the alcoholic intake of sailors in ships, its relation to the breathalyser figures and its long term effects upon men after they left the Navy.

'The results were quite startling, and the figures and reports were sent to the Admiralty with a strong recommendation that the board should take the bull by the horns and abolish the rum issue.

'Writing from memory some of the matters which came to light were:

(a) The tot was equivalent to about three to four pub gins daily.

(b) Taken with a pint of the rather strong tinned beer available overseas it put a sailor over the breathalyser limit.

(c) In at least one frigate the average daily alcoholic intake of the petty officers exceeded one bottle of gin.

(d) Punishment returns showed that nearly all cases of grave indiscipline (contempt, striking, skulking, etc) occurred after rather than before the rum issue.

(e) The number of cases in Netley (psychiatric hospital) attributed to alcohol was higher in proportion to numbers borne for the navy than the other services.

(f) Chief and petty officers were bottling much larger amounts of rum than were suspected and keeping it in their lockers.

'Allied to these facts were factors which made navy rum in particular something rather more than a tot or two of spirits. Rum gave rise to a whole code of practice ranging from "sippers" and "gulpers" to a form of currency, a means of purchasing a relief for duty or a favour; and such favours could be from a dockyard worker for "rabbits" or a lead in to sexual misdemeanours. While the value put on the tot for the "T" man was threepence, its market value in the pub was by 1965 rather nearer five shillings. On top of all this the storage, distribution and accounting for rum, whether in the victualling yards or by the victualling staff afloat, required an immense amount of work particularly in manpower resources. Lastly it should be mentioned that the fact that only the navy of the three services enjoyed the privilege of a daily rum issue was constantly brought up in inter-service discussions on pay or conditions as a perk for which some compensation should be granted to the Army and the Air Force.

'Somewhere about 1967 the abolition of the rum issue came to a head in The Admiralty and a paper to the board was put forward by Vice Admiral Hill-Norton proposing a way to abolish the tot. At this time there was much argument as to how the rum issue could be abolished in the face of the Treasury insistence that no more than the threepence given to the non rum taker could be given. (In fact the cost of a tot was marginally less than threepence.) Such a sum could in no way be used to provide a substitute, such as beer. One school of thought backed the gradual abolition of first by stopping its supply in shore establishments and then by not providing rum for all new entries. But the disadvantages of this plan were that it was so gradual that it would take up to twenty-five years or so to phase out the last rum drinker and the comparison between "entitled" and "non entitled" would keep the rum tradition rumbling along for years.

'Others favoured a simple stop date and others concluded that the traditions and even the appeal of the navy would be far more injured by abolition than by retention. For my part I made a point in my few years at sea as a flag officer, that the rum issue was now an evil which sensible people could see should be abolished; and I did not hesitate to voice this opinion in messes I visited in ships or ashore or in talking with ratings or officers. Although I, naturally, was taken much to task by ratings, and in particular senior ratings, largely on grounds of tradition, mystique and the "manliness" argument, yet I was surprised at the very considerable and balanced support there was for the argument that the breathalyser had put the skids under rum and it was indeed necessary in principle to overcome this situation, particularly if some substitute could be offered.

At this point I became Second Sea Lord and inherited the paper written by Admiral Hill-Norton (who had been my second in command and was holding the fort as Second Sea Lord until I became available), the contents of which had been communicated to me at the time of preparation.

'I decided in my mind that two principles were essential if we were to abolish rum and avoid serious reaction from the lower deck. The first was that it would have to go in one act — chop — and no lingering vestiges; second that some worthwhile compensation must be offered in return for abolition. It was the second factor which was the real difficulty.

'It was appreciated that the money available would not provide any alcoholic substitute and hence the compensation would have to be found in some other area.

'Looking at the matter of alcohol as a whole, certain oddities were apparent in the navy. While we were content to give every man a daily midday drink of say three gins, we were not giving chief and petty officers freedom to buy spirits in their messes afloat — only beer in largish quantities. The privilege of a full bar service was reserved for officers; yet chief petty officers, and in particular the fleet chief petty officer, was very close to being an officer and indeed was a warrant officer. Pre-war warrant officers had full bar facilities.'

Ashore it was different. NAAFI bars sold everything; rum also was issued and even where the sale of spirits was restricted, chief and petty officers in particular could easily go round to the nearest pub.

All this had led to increasing pressure from chief and petty officers to be allowed full bars, if not all the time, at least for entertaining. In turn chief and petty officers' entertainment onboard, which on foreign visits was rapidly paralleling the wardroom official cocktail party, were frequently provided with wines by the wardroom.

'It came to my mind that were the board to trust chief, and perhaps petty officers as well, to act responsibly and to run their bars under no less strict supervision and accountability than the wardroom bar, it might be sensible to allow chief and petty officers to have their own bars in ships where they could purchase spirits (but not also receive a free tot of rum). The rules for bars, the daily amount an individual could purchase and the cost of buying the drink would together reduce the amount of drunkenness onboard which rum had occasioned. And here was a "compensation" of considerable prestige for chief and petty officers if they accepted abolition of the rum issue.

'This left leading hands and below. It had to be recognised that a ship could not carry the stock to make it possible for junior rates to drink and pay as they wished. Beer was already available for them to purchase and it might be that the times and method of this issue could be made more convenient.

'Also the number of junior rates who were staying in the navy to make a long service career after twenty (the age for receiving the tot) was dwindling and the brighter ones could reach petty officer rank much younger than had been possible even a few years back. So it seemed that something must be found to compensate junior sailors if they lost their rum, but not in the line of drink.

118

'By this time in the evolution of a solution, it had been discovered that abolition of rum would save the Navy Vote in three places. First the actual cost of purchasing and importing rum from the West Indies. Second in the cost of the labour force needed to handle the rum in store, the provision of barrels and coopers to mend the barrels, the transport, storage space, accounting and so forth. Lastly the cost (albeit somewhat hidden) of the supply assistants who received and issued the rum ration and dealt with the detailed administration of matters like stopped tots, watchkeepers, 'G' and 'T' and so on. It was reckoned that in a carrier probably at least two men were required whole time on account of rum.

'The estimated cash value of all this infrastructure was of the order of £300,000 a year in 1968. If the Treasury would agree to give sailors £300,000 a year in return for the total abolition of rum, would this not provide a tempting compensation? It seemed worth a try though it also seemed a frail chance.

'Discussion with Sir Michael Carey, the Naval Permanent Secretary, showed that there were dangers in an annual payment even if, as seemed highly unlikely, it was acceptable to the Treasury. First the sum, in the light of inflation, would become worth less and less and second it would become too easily subject to political pressure in times of economic stringency.

'All in all it looked as if the best solution would be a lump sum to be invested in a public charitable trust fund to be run by the sailor for the sailor. Why not invite the Treasury to amortise the rum issue over ten years by a down payment of £3 million to put into this trust fund?

'So the final paper to the board emerged. For myself I felt there was little chance of getting £3m and I could imagine the Treasury saying more like £250,000 — and that was hardly sufficient to meet the compensation needed. However Michael Carey with enormous skill set to work to see what could be done. Before long he told me that he had arranged a meeting with the top Treasury officials at which I was to put the case for a ten year amortization of rum for £3m.

'We duly went over to the Treasury where in the course of some thirty minutes agreement was reached to provide £2.7m for the abolition of rum and this sum would be used to form a trust for the benefit of sailors in the navy. In my wildest dreams I had hardly expected such a large sum to be agreed in such a brief meeting. But there it was — and for this much credit must go the skill of Michael Carey.

'In due course the details for the abolition scheme were hammered out and put to the Board of Admiralty and later to the commanders-in-chief and senior flag officers in command.

'The essence was:

'Abolition of the rum issue.

'Full bars under supervision (not less than that for wardroom bars) to be available to chief and petty officers.

'Setting up of a fund to be called the Sailors' Fund of £2.7m to provide amenities for the lower deck which could not be funded by Defence votes.

'The Sailors' Fund to be managed by the lower deck, its investment being put in the hands of an appropriate merchant or other bank. The capital to be in trust and the income paid out annually.

'Abolition was to be promulgated by a general signal immediately (December 1969) followed by an announcement in Fleet Orders (April 1970). Abolition day was to be in August 1970.

'Dr David Owen and Mr Denis Healey with considerable courage agreed the idea. Under the leadership of Admiral Le Fanu, First Sea Lord, this very important measure was prepared, published, and carried thorugh in what might be called a remarkably short but tense period. The Board was asked whether the navy would mutiny. They answered that in their opinion the discipline, good sense and loyalty of the lower deck would accept this painful and sad decision.

'They proved right. With enormous dignity and plenty of good lower deck fun and poking charley the great issue went through. A naval tradition had been given up. Some said the decision was wrong but most realised it had to be. Splice the main-brace was retained, but for generations Up Spirits will remain a happy memory of the old navy.

' "It don't blow like it used to." '

The rum saga had not quite ended. Existing rum stocks had to be run down so that space could be freed for the extra beer which would have to be embarked in readiness for August 1. Arrangements had to be made also for the storage of sacramental wine which normally lodged with its unlikely bedfellow, rum, in the spirit room!

It would all take time.

You soothed my nerves
    and warmed my limbs
    And cheered my dismal heart
Procured my wants, obliged my whims —
    And now it's time to part

And so the time has come old friend
    To take the final sup
Our tears are shed. This is the end
    Goodbye and bottoms up!

CHAPTER SEVEN

Requiem

THE SHOCK WAVES quickly passed, and with few exceptions naval men accepted the decision's inevitability. Indeed, many looked forward to the alcoholic refreshment which would replace the old rum issue. On January 28, 1970, the Great Rum Debate took place in the House of Commons. Understandably those members with previous naval service, and others elected to represent constituencies with large naval populations, were vociferous in condemning the decision. 'Anger at end of rum issue', said *The Times* headline on January 29, but the promoters of abolition stood their ground and as it turned out the debate was merely political and without much rancour.

Later that year a general election brought in a new government which reviewed the decision. But the Under Secretary for the Navy was able to announce in the Commons, 'I am convinced tha the change is necessary in the light of conditions in the modern navy and that a reversal would not be justified.' The last shot had been fired; rum's time was running out.

On July 30, 1970, the *Daily Express*, which had tended to champion the retention of rum, spearheaded the publicity which the national dailies gave to Black Tot Day — as it became known in the navy. 'That last tot and the Navy's spirits fall', read a headline, commenting that, 'Tomorrow Friday, July 31, 1970, will be for ever remembered in the history of the Royal Navy. The daily routine pipe of Up Spirits is due to sound for the last time.'

The fleet, determined to make it a day to remember, planned to mourn the occasion fittingly with that highly developed sense of histrionics peculiar to the navy. Portsmouth, Chatham and

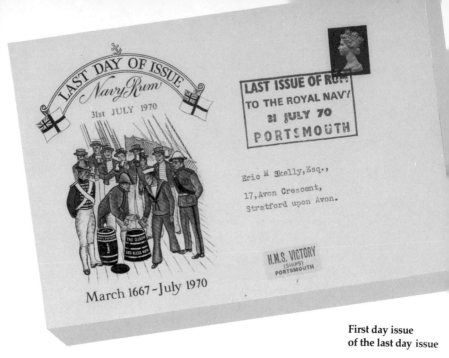

First day issue
of the last day issue

Devonport were the main centres for paying the last rites to the departing 'spirit', and the *Portsmouth Evening News* recorded on July 31, that, 'sailors in ships and establishments in the area buried the rum tot today. They said farewell to the last issue of Nelson's Blood by conducting mock funerals and wearing black armbands. . . . The annual Christmas pudding stirring ceremony in *HMS Bellerophon* was brought forward today so that the usual four pints of rum could be included in the 150lb mix.'

The Post Office was persuaded that the occasion deserved a special hand stamp which was made available at the Portsmouth General Post Office. 'Last Issue of Rum in the Royal Navy July 31, 1970' was the message conveyed. These have now become collectors' items.

Overseas, too, due respects were paid. At *HMS Jufair* a 'stone frigate' in the Persian Gulf, even the establishment's chaplain took part in a specially written committal service, praying that it wasn't blasphemous. A rum barrel with a headstone bearing a suitable epitaph was interred with the words, 'For as much as it hath pleased the Lord High Admirals to take away from us the issue of our dearly beloved tot, we therefore commit its cask to the ground, sip to sip, splashes to splashes, thirst to thirst, in the sure and certain knowledge that it will never again be restored to us, but with the glorious hope that it might be according to the mighty working whereby MOD (Navy) is able to accomplish all things unto itself.'

Afloat, the most outstanding privilege fell to the guided missile destroyer *HMS Fife* which, being at Pearl Harbour and close to the international date line at the time, made the last regulation Up Spirits call to be heard anywhere in the world. The grog issue was observed with exaggerated pomp and circumstance. On the ship's small flight deck American television cameras recorded the event. The rum tub of shining oak, with brightly polished lettering on its side, provided evidence of an affectionate preparation for its final duty. Slowly the ship's company began to muster, many sporting black arm bands. Some were dressed in drab mourning clothes and even Long John Silver was there with a lifeless parrot on his shoulder. This pleased the cameramen but the American reporters by their questioning, 'What's all this fuss over a glass of rum?' obviously found it difficult to comprehend what the rum issue had meant to the British Navy.

As noon approached (Hawaiian time), a lament was played on the pipes and the men silently formed a queue by the tub. Suddenly the call came over the broadcast, 'Secure. Hands to dinner, rum issue is now taking place on the flight deck.'

Under the eye of the officer of the day the issue began, and as tots were consumed, so the tot glasses were thrown over the ship's side in a mock gesture of farewell. When all was over, the rum breaker itself was carried aft and committed to a watery grave to the accompaniment of a twenty-one gun salute. The end of this long tradition saddened the hearts of many.

Even civilians took part in the obsequies. During the afternoon performance of the Royal Tournament at Earl's Court on July 31, 1970, the announcer, in grave tones, told the audience that on this day the rum issue, a daily privilege enjoyed for centuries, had ended but that the Royal Navy wished to mark the occasion suitably.

The doors of the arena were thrown open, and to the accompaniment of the *Dead March in Saul,* there appeared a sailor mounted on the Household Brigade drum horse and beating out the slow march in time with the band ahead of a funeral cortege. He wore a broad black sash over his white uniform. There followed a funeral firing party with arms reversed and a gun carriage drawn by sailors, on which were assembled a grog tub and the copper measures used in the issue.

The mourners were sailors dressed in rigs traditional to seamen during the centuries in which rum had been issued.

As their cortege approached the Royal Box, reversed arms were sloped and the band struck up a lively tune. On the salute, the Inspecting Officer raised a glass of brown liquid and drank to the health of the mourners and their lost privilege. It was, in fact, Coca Cola!

The late Admiral of the Fleet Sir Michael Le Fanu — First Sea Lord in 1970 and a man loved by all — issued the final decree for rum to cease and gave a press interview.

'I'm not expecting to rocket to top of the pops in the navy on this,' was his characteristic comment to those present, but the understanding with which the fleet accepted the decision was his deserved reward. He had a fair complexion and the navy, never short of the *mot juste,* called him 'Dry Ginger' thereafter.

Paradoxically, although the long history of rum in the Royal Navy ended with Black Tot Day, an afterglow helps to keep the tradition alive and in the minds of seamen.

The most obvious is the Sailors' Fund which has now been operating successfully for the benefit of ratings and Royal Marine other ranks, for more than a decade, under a committee representing the various naval commands. The fund's origins are well known through the more familiar title of the Tot Fund as the fleet calls it. Already it has disbursed considerable sums of money on capital projects for the improvement of living conditions and amenities in general.

Should men be required to undertake particularly arduous service, the rules permit a commanding officer to authorise a daily ration of one eighth of a pint of spirit, provided that in his opinion there is a medical requirement for it, just as in the army. Splicing the main-brace which is explained later, has also been retained and continues as a link with ancient custom.

The rum itself was made to a complicated blend difficult to duplicate without the formula which was still held by the

Admiral of the Fleet Sir Michael Le Fanu, who was First Sea Lord and ultimately responsible when the issue of rum was abolished

Admiralty. With the disposal of all Admiralty rum stocks after 1970, it seemed that this special rum, issued at 95.5 proof, was gone forever. Admiralty rum, or 'Pusser's' as it was often called, was said by connoisseurs to have a flavour and smoothness which was unsurpassed by any other.

Fortunately, Mr Charles Tobias, an ex-US Marine and a successful businessman, was so fired by the romance of British naval rum that he decided, if possible, to recreate it. With the enthusiastic support of E D & F Man, the long-standing rum brokers to the Admiralty, and with the full co-operation and encouragement of the Admiralty Board, he obtained the formula of the rum that had so long fortified the spirit of the jack tars of the Royal Navy.

Having formed his own company — Pusser's Ltd — in partnership with E D & F Man, he built his own blending and bottling plant on the small and beautiful island of Tortola in the Crown Colony of the British Virgin Islands. Pusser's Rum was launched commercially in 1980, exactly ten years after its withdrawal from the Royal Navy.

Charles Tobias decided that for every case of Pusser's Rum sold, a royalty donation of two American dollars would always be given to the Royal Navy Sailors' Fund, which generous apportionment of profits has already resulted in large sums accruing to it. Through his efforts he had provided, it might be said, not only atonement for the darker side of the rum story, but also a direct link between Pusser's Rum and the Royal Navy.

Admiral Tait, Second Sea Lord, receiving a cheque for the Sailors' Fund from Mr Charles Tobias

*C onvinced after a year's
reflection that the cause
of both temperance and
democracy demanded it,
I issued General Order 99'*

Josephus Daniels
Secretary of the Navy
on introducing prohibition
in the US Navy 1914

CHAPTER EIGHT

The American connection

AMERICANS CAN BOAST just as intimate a connection with Admiral Edward Vernon, the inventor of grog, as the British themselves. During the War of Jenkins' Ear in the campaign commanded by Vernon against the Spanish Main, the North American colonies furnished 3,000 volunteers, who for the first time were called Americans instead of Provincials. Serving with them was Lawrence Washington, older brother of George who, upon returning to Virginia, created his plantation which he named Mount Vernon after the Admiral. It is certain that the many Americans who served in the Royal Navy during the colonial period became accustomed to the grog ration instituted in 1740, no less than their British cousins.

Among the first rules for the regulation of the American Continental Navy established to fight the War of Independence was one providing for the issue of 'half a pint of rum per man every day, and a discretionary allowance for extra duty and in time of engagement'. These rules were formally adopted by the Congress sitting at Philadelphia on November 28, 1775.

Rum was no stranger to the American mainland as for many years it had been distilled in New England from molasses imported from the West Indies. In the capture of Louisbourg as far back as 1746, New Englanders sold their rum to the British troops in vast quantity, and even raised recruits from Newfoundland by sending a cargo of rum there. After the second capture of Louisbourg in 1758 the British general, temporarily on station with his troops in Boston, recorded with resignation after the victory that 'the jubilation was so exuberant that I could not prevent the men from being quite filled with rum by the inhabitants'. But nobody minded!

There is little doubt that rum's cheapness and over-availability was a cause of the increasing friction between the 'bloodybacks' of the garrison and the Sons of Liberty manifested by the events at Lexington and Concord. The outbreak of the revolution limited the import of molasses, but ample stocks of local rum for issuing to the troops were still available. The debacle at Trenton on Christmas Day of 1776, when thirteen hundred Hessian mercenaries in the employ of the British were overcome by Washington's daring raid, was largely attributable to celebrating Yuletide not wisely but too well.

Could rum have been a factor in the loss of the American colonies? It would be wrong to attribute such significance to it but, unlike other warlike occasions when a regulated issue proved of value, no such praise can be awarded to 'red-eye' in North America.

At the end of the war the US Navy was dissolved to be re-established in 1794 because of the actions of the Barbary pirates in the Mediterranean. Now an act of Congress included in the navy's rations 'one half pint of distilled spirits per day, or in lieu thereof, one quart of beer per day'. Splicing the main-brace also became a popular custom in the navy of the new nation.

The first published naval US regulations, in 1802, ordered the captain of a ship of war 'not to suffer any person to suttle or sell any sort of liquors to the ship's company'. This indicated that the US Navy had the same troubles as HM ships suffered at the hands of bumboatmen in harbour. Much care was taken therefore in the stowage of spirits in naval vessels; the spirit room in the after-hold was kept locked at all times except for the daily serving. The ritual employed in issuing the grog ration bore striking similarity to that in the Royal Navy. At seven bells under charge of the master's mate the brew was pumped from the cask in the spirit room into a covered wooden grog tub. A chaplain onboard *USS Constitution* (Old Ironsides), in the early nineteenth century described such an occasion, 'Shortly after eight bells, as the drum rolls, all move aft, towards the grog tub. Around this point of time concentrate half the meditations of the day. I often place myself at the tub, to watch the rolling eyes, and the look of supreme gratification with which they swallow their half pint; for that is the measure to each; it is one gill of whiskey

The bombardment of St Jean d'Acre, 1840 when steamships were in action for the first time, including HMS Gorgon (see page 80)

Have I been cheated?
The Purser, alias
Mr Nipcheese,
checking his rum
receipts

diluted with an equal quantity of water. A rope is drawn athwartships, near the tub; each as his name is called, and crossed, takes his allowance which must be drunk on the spot. From this, they pass to dinner. The whole operation is superintended by the officer of the deck.'

In 1806, the Navy Department tried substituting whiskey for rum as an economy measure after 'being persuaded that it is a more wholesome drink'. The sailors, however, continued to prefer rum and it was some years before whiskey became more acceptable. Rear Admiral Oscar W Farenholt recalled the grog ration aboard *USS Wabash* in 1862, as being 'a straight rye, generally come from distilleries at Pittsburgh, and was called Monongahela'. It was delivered in twenty-gallon barrels and cost a dollar ten cents per gallon.

The first attempt to restrict the grog ration came in a congressional resolution of 1829 which directed the Secretary of the Navy to appoint three surgeons to investigate the necessity and expediency of distilled spirits as part of the rations allowed midshipmen and to comment on the effect of spirits on the health and morals of the young men. The panel of surgeons agreed that the ration was unnecessary, inexpedient and demoralising. Although Navy Secretary John Branch favoured temperance, no prohibition law was passed, and the Secretary had to be satisfied by issuing orders that those in the naval service could voluntarily relinquish their spirit ration and be paid five cents per ration for a period of not less than a month. By 1862, Admiral Farenholt reported 'more than one half of the 480 men in the *Wabash* had their spirit rations commuted, and this was about average in all of our ships at that time'.

A restriction was placed on the number of spirit rations allowed officers in 1835, limiting them to one per day. Previously an officer had been entitled to rations based on his rank — a captain as many as six, a commander five, and so on.

In 1842, the ration was reduced to a gill of spirits or half a pint of wine per man per day (while the Royal Navy reduced to a gill in 1824, and half a gill of spirits in 1850). Further, all personnel under twenty-one years of age were to be given extra pay per day in lieu of the grog ration.

Early in 1850, the Navy Department asked all commanding officers to report their opinions on the use of corporal punishment and the spirit ration. Comment was divided, but soon both flogging and grog were abolished. Individual officers had mixed opinions on the use of distilled spirits. Paymaster William F Keeler, who served in *USS Monitor* in the famous first clash of ironclad ships, wrote, 'Once during the fight I opened the spirit room by order of Captain Worden and dealt to each man a gill of whiskey, and if liquor ever does good to anyone and is ever useful, it must be on some such occasion.' A month later Keeler wrote in a letter to his wife, 'There are three great evils in both our army and navy which if corrected would render them more efficient — the first is whiskey, the second is whiskey, and the third is whiskey. If this evil spirit was banished entirely from our land and sea forces it would add ten per cent to their strength and efficiency, while it would decrease in a much greater ratio the number in the hospitals.'

James Dobbin, Navy Secretary under President Franklin Peirce, had promoted temperance. Finally, President Lincoln's Assistant Secretary of the Navy — Gustavus V Fox — persuaded Senator James Grimes of Iowa to introduce a bill in Congress to end the issuing of grog in the American Navy. On July 14, 1862, Congress resolved that 'the spirit ration shall forever cease and thereafter no distilled spiritous liquor shall be admitted onboard vessels of war, except as medicine and upon the order and under the control of the medical officer and to be used only for medical purposes.'

Mr Lincoln confirmed the resolution and ordered the grog ration to end on September 1, 1862, wishing at the same time that 'he could give the same drastic order for the army' which had no liquor ration but carried whiskey in its supplies.

To lament the passing of the old established custom, Paymaster Caspar Schenck serving aboard *USS Portsmouth* on the Mississippi river composed a ditty to be sung in the wardroom on August 31, 1862 (shades of Black Tot Day in the Royal Navy),

> Farewell to Grog
> Oh! messmates, pass the bottle round,
> Our time is short remember,
> For our grog must stop and our spirits drop,
> On the first day of September.
>
> *Chorus*
> For tonight we'll merry, merry be,
> For tonight we'll merry, merry be,

For tonight we'll merry, merry be,
Tomorrow we'll be sober.

Farewell, old rye! 'tis a sad, sad world,
But alas it must be spoken;
The ruby cup must be given up;
And the demijohn be broken.

Jack's happy days will soon be past,
To return again, no, never
For they've raised his pay five cents a day
And stopped his grog forever.

Yet memory oft will backward turn,
And dwell with fondness partial,
On the plays when gin was not a sin,
Nor cocktails brought courts-martial.

All hands to splice the main-brace call,
But splice it now in sorrow,
For the spirit room key will be laid away,
Forever, on the morrow.

The law of 1862 did not end the grog ration in all American naval vessels, nor did it prohibit the storing or consumption of alcoholic beverages in any man-of-war. The Confederate States Navy continued to issue grog and their commerce raider *CSS Shenandoah*, which fought on in 1865 unaware the war had ended, was probably the last American vessel to use the grog tub officially. Spirits were still allowed in medical stores and, more significantly, in the officers' wardroom and captain's mess.

According to Hamersly's *Naval Encyclopaedia*, in 1881, officers were permitted 'fermented drinks but not spirituous liquors'. The wardrooms were supposed to stock only wine and beer. To circumvent this limitation, some ships labelled their scotch as 'wine A' and their bourbon as 'wine B'. It also became a custom to extend an invitation to a fellow officer for cocktails by having a mess boy deliver a broken wooden match. Some wardrooms were even provisioned with elaborate and beautiful services of crystal glass stemware and decanters for use in their messes — but whether these were provided officially or by wine merchants keen to solicit custom is in some doubt.

By 1900, the temperance movement in the United States which had begun in the early nineteenth century had gained political strength among 'progressives'. The Navy Secretary John D Long issued an order prohibiting the sale or issue to enlisted men of any alcoholic beverage in ships or at shore stations. This made it unfair on these men who were expected to carry supplies onboard for the officers, when they themselves were severely punished if caught with a beer of their own.

Finally in April 1914, Josephus Daniels, a teetotaller and 'country hick' from North Carolina as he seemed to many in the navy, took the sensational step of imposing total prohibition when serving as Secretary of the Navy to Woodrow Wilson. 'Convinced after a year's reflection that the cause of both temperance and democracy demanded it,' Daniels later wrote, 'I issued General Order 99.' This read,

'On July 1, 1914, Article 827, *Naval Instructions* will be annulled, and in its stead the following will be substituted: The use or introduction for drinking purposes of alcoholic liquors on board any naval vessel or within any navy yard or station, is strictly prohibited, and commanding officers will be held directly responsible for the enforcement of this order.'

Needless to say, Daniel's popularity and support among naval officers withered, and he was lampooned in the press. One cartoon depicted Daniels as 'Sir Josephus, Admiral of USS *Grapejuice Pinafore'*. Another included a parody on a naval song,

> Away, away, with sword and drum,
> Here we come, full of rum
> Looking for something to put on the bum
> In the Armoured Cruiser Squadron.

> Josephus Daniels is a goose,
> If he thinks he can induce
> Us to drink his damn grape juice
> In the Armoured Cruiser Squadron.

Daniels, however, had the endorsement of President Wilson as well as the progressive movement. When he issued his order, he also released a strong statement from the Navy's Surgeon General who declared that shipboard wine messes impaired the 'clear head and steady hand' the navy needed.

Also coming very much to Daniels' aid was a crisis in Mexico which captured the headlines a few weeks after he had announced his decision; this required a large part of the US Atlantic fleet to proceed to the Gulf of Mexico. It was here off Vera Cruz on the evening of June 30, 1914, that the fleet had to dispose of its remaining stores of distilled spirits. Officers and the press corps took it in their stride, and General Order 99 became an invitation to one of the largest cocktail parties ever held, at this, the legal ending to the drinking of distilled spirits aboard American naval vessels of war.

Thirty years later, by which time the United States Navy had become well accustomed to its 'dry' state, the exigencies of war brought American servicemen into close contact with their British allies. By occasionally sharing mess life aboard British warships, or on joint operations, Americans could see how the other half lived with the long lost drinking habit which they had finally surrendered in 1914.

Any American who might be witnessing the grog issue for the first time, tended to be dazzled by the event. 'Strange people these Limeys' would have been his secret thoughts. A British seaman, Mr J Hamilton of Luton while serving in the Mediterranean provides the following account, 'Aboard HMS Glasgow flagship of Lord Louis Mountbatten, I was rum bos'n for number five mess. One day two American servicemen who had been invited aboard, watched the mess mustering for their rum when the ceremony was in full swing. It was obvious that they had seen nothing like it before — their faces showed it! Later in the mess, they witnessed the sailors coming down for their tots. I offered "gulpers" to the two Americans. Their eyes watered, a sure sign they were tasting Pusser's rum for the first time. "Geeze, no wonder you guys fight like pirates, you live like pirates",' pronounced one of them.

Once the first astonishment was over, reactions varied from approval to disgust. For many Americans 'Barbados waters' had no attraction at all, as Mr N Barnett of Bristol relates, 'Serving aboard HMS Russell in winter, we were ordered to Reykjavik to embark a US Air Force helicopter, crew and maintenance personnel to rescue an injured crew member of a ship locked in the Greenland ice. Some of the American personnel were billeted in our mess in very cramped surroundings. The Arctic weather on passage was appalling. As mess rum bos'n I drew extra rations for our new American messmates but feeling the effects of the ship rolling and tossing, they soon took to their hammocks. Up Spirits was piped and I offered one of our American buddies his tot. He asked me to do him a great favour. If he had "sippers" would I drink the rest and not tell the others that he hadn't drunk it. "That's against naval regulations," I said, "but if *you* don't tell anyone, I'll drink it as a special favour." They were with us for nearly two weeks and I secretly spliced the main-brace every day. I still secretly splice the main-brace when my wife isn't looking.'

Again, when America and Britain had embarked upon the biggest landing invasion of all time Mr P Lund of Cheadle writes, ' "A tot of rum is to be issued to every man before going ashore." So said the orders for Operation Neptune, the naval side of Operation Overlord for the invasion of Normandy. At this time, I was first lieutenant of Landing Craft Tank 709, and it was my duty to dish out the rum. When we began to ferry ashore the Americans, we found that they did not think much of the rum, "What's this son of a bitch stuff?" one said as he tossed it over the side!'

There were occasions when sheer necessity forced even British warships to become dry — catastrophic for those British naval ratings who were compelled to endure without their rum. At such moments the Americans had the whip hand as Mr F Pearce of Bristol, in his story of the Normandy landings, makes clear, 'Two old British light cruisers, the *Capetown* and the *Ceres* came under American control but still flew the White Ensign. On April 5, 1944, they were taken out of "rotten row" in Devonport and came alongside in the yard. I joined the *Capetown* whose ship's company consisted of approximately half RN and half USN personnel, with two captains, one from each service. Operational command was exercised by the USN so the RN contingent lost its tot privileges. Even the wardroom was dry!

'By September, the allied foothold in France was secure and we returned to Devonport where the USN personnel were to leave ship. Our first lieutenant announced that provided the Americans were out of the ship by 1000 there would be an issue of rum. Never before has there been so much assistance offered to the "Gobs" as that morning with the RN matelots carrying their kit and ensuring all their belongings were landed safely on

Stan Laurel of Hollywood fame joins the rum queue in HMS Dolphin, 1947 (by permission of Lieutenant-Commander R Swift)

the jetty. As soon as they had cleared the jetty Up Spirits was piped (supplies being already aboard), and the cheer that went up could be heard the length of the yard. Our first tot for almost six months was nectar!'

But British naval rum was not universally distasteful to American palates, as this story from Mr J. Harwood of Leicester proves, 'At Easter 1946, I was a supernumerary in *HMS Phoenicia,* Sliema, Malta. An immediate draft came through giving me just forty-five minutes to collect my gear and join an LST due to sail to Taranto in Italy. In packing I noticed a sealed gallon stone jar beside my locker, which turned out to be rum. Who had left it, or why, I never discovered. I packed it carefully in the centre of my kit bag, and joined the LST which sailed immediately. The draft was to a small unit in Taranto involved in packing and shipping recoverable stores and equipment from the minesweeper base there. As I was under-age to draw rum, I decided not to mention my find.

'Our group was billeted near a US Army supply depot where American stores and equipment left over from the war were also being cleared. Within days I was a regular visitor to the depot both on and off duty and noticed a Jeep with a damaged windscreen but with a bare thirty miles on the speedometer. After exchanging tins of corned beef for tins of sausage meat with the friendly American staff sergeant in charge, I asked him if he liked rum.

' "Yes," was his immediate reply. Suggesting that perhaps I could get hold of a reasonable quantity he showed interest and demanded my price.

' "The Jeep for a gallon of rum," I replied, to which he agreed saying that he would not only swap the Jeep, but give it a new windscreen as well.

'Next day I drove the Jeep back to the billet and told the officer-in-charge that I had acquired it but not how it had been obtained. An Australian with no time for red tape he readily agreed to my keeping it provided he could borrow it if needed. He arranged petrol and made me its driver. In August 1946, we were drafted back to *HMS Phoenicia* taking the Jeep with us, where it was placed in a nearby motor transport park. I drove over Malta many times but was never questioned on whose authority I was driving it. In January 1948, I returned to the UK for demobilisation. I have often wondered what happened to the Jeep. After all, it was my very first car.'

For grog is our starboard,
our larboard
Our mainmast, our mizzen
our log —
At sea or ashore, or when harbour'd
The Mariner's compass is grog

CHAPTER NINE

The daily ritual

THE CEREMONY OF UP SPIRITS and the daily issue of rum and grog in the Royal Navy, had followed a familiar pattern for two centuries before its abolition in 1970, but as with any long-standing custom, expediency had demanded changes. Its origins date back to 1740, with Admiral Vernon's order which gave birth to the ceremony, '. . . and to be mixed in a scuttled butt kept for that purpose, and to be done upon deck in the presence of the lieutenant of the watch, who is to take particular care to see that the men are not defrauded in having their full allowance of rum, and when so mixed is to be served to them in two servings in the day, the one between the hours of ten and twelve in the morning, and the other between four and six in the afternoon'.

It took a considerable time for the Navy Board to confirm Vernon's order: sixteen years to be precise and as an addition to *The Regulations and Instructions Relating to His Majesty's Service at Sea* (first published in 1731). But this was not unusual; communication was unreliable and slow, and Vernon's instructions, of course, applied only to ships on the West Indies station. The Navy Board's order was made in the following somewhat forbidding tones, 'And whereas it is of very pernicious consequence to suffer the seamen to drink in drams the allowance made to them of any kind of spirituous liquor in lieu of beer and it having been found by experience, that the serving it mixed with water is very conducive to the preservation of their health; every commander is therefore strictly charged, never to suffer any kind of spirituous liquor to be issued by itself, to the company of the ship or vessel under his command, but to cause the allowance for all the officers and company, to be every day mixed with a due proportion of water upon deck, in the presence of the lieutenant and two other officers of the watch who are to be strictly charged to take care that the men are not defrauded in their allowance. . . .'

Their Lordships were always insistent about 'no drams' — or, in other words, no neat spirit. Later they were to concede that chief petty officers, and then petty officers as well, should be entitled to draw their rum neat. However this did not occur until the latter half of the nineteenth century by which time the daily ration had been reduced to an eighth of a pint of rum. 'No drams' when it stood at half a pint a day of 'neaters' is not too surprising an edict.

From Vernon's time to the end of the Napoleonic Wars, two issues of grog per day remained the custom whenever beer was unavailable. But the use of rum gradually became more widespread as did the issuing ritual which went with it.

In Nelson's day, the ship's fiddler or fifer played an important part in announcing the rum issue. The favourite air, *Nancy Dawson*, would be the signal for cooks of messes to repair to the rum tub to draw rations for their messmates. The morning issue at twelve o'clock constituted the most pleasant part of the day as the ration had been well earned by a hard forenoon's work. It was the second issue in the evening which caused most of the trouble, as has been noted.

After the introduction of long service in the 1850's, the men themselves became much more wedded to the navy and more professional in their outlook. To them, the single daily issue of rum which it had now become, was so much a part of their lives as to create for it a marked mystique. The regulations concerning rum proliferated — as they had to if abuses were to be prevented. The daily ritual itself was as foolproof as it could be, but Jack was ever one to discover loopholes.

The individual with the greatest responsibility aboard was the stores assistant who had to maintain the daily book-keeping and account for the quantities of rum issued; the acknowledged expert, known to all and sundry as Jack Dusty, his was a name handed down from the early days when Jack of the Dust was the appellation for the purser's steward employed in the breadroom.

Jack Dusty's assistant was usually a seaman, or sometimes the Royal Marine butcher if the ship carried a Marine detachment. His contribution was the physical one of fetching, carrying, stirring the grog and doling out, an assignment requiring a type who, lacking ambition, yet preferred to work on his own. He was called the Tanky, a name originating from the sailing master's assistant of earlier times whose job was to tend the fresh water tanks and help with the grog issue of those days. His election required discrimination since Tanky could develop into the biggest 'rum rat' of all if he was inclined that way.

Two others were regularly involved in the ritual. The petty officer of the day who was not a full time member of the party but took his turn from a duty roster, and the officer of the day who needs no explanation except that his experience for the task varied widely. As witnessing officer of the ritual daily he was either quick to pick up irregularities, or failed to notice them at all to the delight of those who benefited from his inexperience.

At 10.30 in the morning, according to that ritual which can vary from ship to ship in detail, Jack Dusty is working in the victualling office, poring over his spirit issue book which lists by messes all those borne on the ship's books. His task is to assess the number of those entitled to draw their spirit that day. Those who are temperance or under-age, of course, are excluded, but he has also to allow for men stopped grog as well as for the gangway victualling and check sheets, provided by the regulating office, which report that day's movements of men in and out of ship. Having juggled with his figures for some while, he produces an overall total for the day's issue together with the amounts for each mess, a proficiency acquired only by constant repetition.

Six Bells are followed by the shrill whistle of the boatswain's call. Up Spirits intones the boatswain's mate, answered by a chorus — *sotto voce* of Stand Fast the Holy Ghost from the throats of those throughout the ship who are eagerly awaiting the lower deck's main social event of the day.

Next, the officer of the day is rounded up by the petty officer of the day who politely reminds him that it is time for Up Spirits, firmly ushering him to the Important key board to draw the keys for both the spirit room and the spirit 'barricoe' pronounced 'breaker' into which the rum is to be poured and conveyed.

Our young officer of the day does not relish his tiresome journey to the spirit room, a compartment below water level reached only be negotiating many ladders and hatches. It is in an area where Damage Control restrictions apply. He is also aware that in witnessing the intricate routine about to take place, he is a pawn in the hands of Tanky whose sleight of hand can deceive even the most experienced eye.

Keys safely drawn, the party makes its way to the spirit room door which is unclipped and unlocked before the four officials enter. The heady vapours which permeate the atmosphere provided an instant understanding of the regulation which forbids the use of naked light — made necessary, no doubt, from a disastrous experience of sailing ship days. Also congregating in the area is a small and motley group of messmen clutching their containers into which will be poured the neat spirit ration for the chief and petty officers messes which they represent. It is the privilege of all senior ratings to draw their one-eighth of a pint of rum neat, and to drink it in their messes ahead of the general issue if they so desire.

In a well-run spirit room as is this, Jack Dusty has ensured sufficient 'ullage' left over from the previous day's issue for the neat allocation to chiefs and petty officers. This having been carried out and recorded in the spirit book, the serious business of broaching a new cask is undertaken. The contents of each cask or barrel is etched on its end; when the bung is removed with a special iron pricker, a broom handle is inserted until it touches the opposite bilge of the cask. Incidentally this cask, along with its neighbours, lies on its side to prevent evaporation through the bung. The broom handle displaces approximately the same volume of rum as the spirit pump shortly to be used, but none spills. The cask is then filled to the bung lip from the remaining ullage, which amount is duly recorded in the 'Required to fill column' of the spirit book, yet another factor Jack Dusty has to take into account in his daily wizardry of balancing the books.

Spirit is then drawn from the cask by means of a single action highly polished copper pump. A skilled operator can make the return valve function at the point of suction so that on removing the pump from a cask, a full pint or more of spirit is trapped in the pump's barrel for later use — or misuse. Officer of the day be on your guard!

The spirit is duly pumped up and measured by means of accurate and handsomely lipped copper measures. The required amount for the day's grog issue is placed in the barricoe or breaker which is then padlocked and taken to the victualling office in readiness for distribution later. The officer of the day

Two early twentieth-century photographs of the issue of grog aboard
HMS Glory (above) and HMS Endymion (below). A Royal Marine Tankie (Glory)
and a Jack Dusty with his accounts (Endymion) are clearly visible

retains the key.

By 11.45 am the grog tub with its splendid brass lettering, *The Queen God Bless Her,* has been set up in the victualling office flat or other convenient spot. Following the age-old naval maxim that, 'them as is keen gets fell in previous', it will be observed that leading from the tub is a short line of rum fannies each bearing its mess number and with some of them containing water which will be used for mixing with the rum. The rum fanny is a round receptacle named after a certain young lady Fanny Adams whose remains were said to have been found after her murder (in the late nineteenth century) in the Deptford victualling yard where experiments were then being carried out in supplying the fleet with preserved mutton. The round tins containing the mutton were used by seamen for drawing their grog and were called fannies from that day forward.

Five minutes later at approximately ten to twelve, 'Cooks to the galley, hands of the mess for rum' is piped by the boatswain's mate on his call and, as though by magic, each fanny is joined by its custodian or Rum Bos'n.

The same little party under the officer of the day meet again by the rum tub where the locked breaker of spirit has been placed. The proceedings are then started by Jack Dusty who informs the officer of the day of the rum stops, another name for those who for various reasons are temporarily out of the ship. The appropriate quantity of rum is taken from the breaker, poured into a bottle, and handed into the charge of the officer of the day who will make arrangements for its issue after 'secure' later in the day. At this time no water is added as grog becomes flat and tasteless within forty-five minutes or so of mixing.

Jack Dusty calls out the quantity of neat spirit remaining in the breaker and as the first step double this amount of water is measured and poured into the tub. This measurement is less accurate than the preceding, and Tanky uses unlipped cup-like measures which allow a generous overspill. By employing this technique not even the last man in the line will go short.

At this stage, an element of time-honoured tradition enters the proceedings. Tanky offers the officer of the day a small measure of water from the tub, uttering at the same time, 'Test for salt, sir'. The latter, having satisfied himself that the water is pure and unsullied, gives a nod, the rum is poured from the breaker into the water in the grog tub, and the mixture is stirred thoroughly.

Splice the Main-brace (flags AD 28) as flown today (from the Allied Maritime Tactical Signal Book)

As flown from pre-war to 1951 (ZTM in the Fleet Signal Book)

BX were the flags flown to indicate splicing the main-brace between 1952 and 1974 (From the Allied Naval Signal and Allied Maritime Tactical Signal Books)

Sailors of the Bellerophon outside their tent in Crimea

'First Mess' is the cry.

'Number Ten Mess' or whatever answers the rum bos'n who is first in line. At the same time he holds his fanny well over the edge of the rum tub ready to receive the mess's ration of grog. The duty petty officer verifies the quantity of grog to be issued and calls it out, while Jack Dusty annotates his spirit book.

'Number Ten Mess, half out of five', is the announcement meaning four and a half pints, the equivalent of twelve rations for the men in that mess at three-eighths of a pint each.

The quickness of the hand can deceive the eye. The rigmarole and language has developed from long custom and is understood only by those taking part. The officer of the day without wishing to show his ignorance may feel that he should stamp his authority upon the issue. He makes an occasional query and sometimes asks for an allowance to be tipped back into the tub and reissued, Tanky and company recognising the transparency of his gesture. Thus the ritual continues until all messes have received their allowance.

'Ditch the ullage?' asks Tanky.

'Yes please,' answers the officer of the day, and the small left-over is emptied from the grog tub over the ship's side. It does not always find its way into the sea but here hangs a tale reserved for a later chapter. The officer of the day signs the spirit book to certify that the quantities of rum shown have been issued, dismisses the party, and proceeds to the wardroom where, before sitting down to lunch, he partakes of his own particular tipple — a pink gin.

Only one element of the ceremony remains after grog has been issued and this is the most important — its drinking. The rum bos'ns repair to their messes with all speed and surefootedness (even in a force ten gale) to distribute the ration among their messmates. Mugs or glasses are set up at the end of each table together with a bakelite measure. Some men are delayed by their duty watch, but there is an unwritten code prevailing so that any tots not drawn immediately are carefully set aside for their owners' return.

Understandably in the chiefs' and petty officers' messes there is a greater informality. For their neat rum, the eighth of a pint lipped jug measure is used. Finer details of distribution are:

1 Select a clean dry glass and half fill it with rum from the

container or rum fanny.

2 Pour from the glass into the tot measure until the glass is empty ensuring all excess rum overflows into the rum jug.

3 Gently pour a little drop extra from the tot measure back into the jug.

4 Pour the contents of the tot measure back into your glass.

5 If you wish to offer any of your messmates a sipper or a gulper, or any other portion of your tot now is the time.

6 What's left you DRINK — only officers and ladies sip!

When the last drops have been drained, the rum fannies and measures are reverently stowed away for the next day. Keep them clean but never let their inner walls be washed is the custom. A story from Mr D Rands of Scunthorpe tells of a leading hand of one mess being seen close to tears.

'What's up?' he was asked.

'What's up?' he said. 'You'll never guess what those daft-so-and-so's in my mess did this morning.'

'What's that?' chorused everyone.

'They've only polished the inside of our rum fanny with blue-bell. There's fifteen tots in there tasting of metal polish and no-one will touch it.'

The story adds that a neighbouring mess, not quite so squeamish, finished it for them.

Lipped jug rum measures (top right); Imperial measures (top left) and one-gallon wicker jars just visible on ground, as used in Gibraltar

'...*Old fish, too cunning
for the hook'*

Crabbe 1754-1832
The Parish Register

CHAPTER TEN
Rum ruses

THAT LITTLE EXTRA — and why not if you can get it? After all, it is a perfectly human reaction which most mortals share, and when that extra relates to such a desirable item as rum, then considerable ingenuity to obtain it is inevitable.

Not that there was much scope for enterprise. The experience of centuries, and a thorough familiarity with tricks of the trade, had long since put authority on its guard. The regulations concerning the handling of rum were tight; if they were rigidly observed little could go wrong. However, there were occasions when they were not — indeed, could not be — strictly enforced, particularly under the stress of war.

There were other factors such as the size of the warship — a coastal motor boat could hardly be expected to adopt the same routine for issuing rum as that of an aircraft carrier. Then, too, there was the human factor — the severity or leniency of those in charge observing the detail of the ritual which made it impossible to maintain common standards. It was against this background that the discerning rum rat had to pit his wits in his quest for that extra.

Not that the game was played with the sole intention of cheating authority. Skulduggery was not unknown but the primary aim was the extraction of small quantities of rum along the issuing line even from messmates, in order to supplement the individual's ration. It was highly professional and *de rigueur* provided a long-established code of conduct was observed.

After the issue of grog from the tub, the ullage as it was called, was thrown over the ship's side or, in a shore establishment, down a convenient drain.

Many and varied were the methods contrived by sailors to prevent what many thought was a flagrant waste of the golden liquid. In olden days at least, it had been habitual to regard the left-over as the cook's perks.

Stories abound — many undoubtedly true and others to be taken with a grain of salt. A practice which was most common, and therefore equally well known by the regulating staff who were on their guard against it, was that of stationing one of Tanky's friends at a scuttle on the ship's side immediately below the disposal point on deck. The idea was to capture in a receptacle the grog which was intended for the sea. But not all witnessing officers were thoroughly versed in the pitfalls, and a green sub lieutenant on duty might be just the opportunity for putting such a plan into execution.

Sometimes grog was issued in the seamen's bathroom flat when the most convenient disposal point for the remains might well be a handy wash-basin. A tale relates how in one ship the normal draining system to the wash-basin used for this purpose was replaced by a sparkling length of new pipework which led straight to a well concealed fanny. For many a day the secret was as well kept as the wash-basin itself which positively sparkled with its daily wipe round.

A couple of true stories might better illustrate the temptation of plushers — as the left-over in the mess was called. The origin of the word was from the French *plus* which then became the over-plus before degenerating into plushers. Mr C H Hobbs of Nottingham writes, 'I was serving as a Petty Officer Cook in HMS *Aurora* in 1943 after the landings at Casablanca, Oran and Algiers. I was on friendly terms with the old time-serving Royal Marine whose duties included ship's butcher and Tanky for the daily rum ration. I noticed that at times he was a bit unsteady on his legs. On duty one day in the ship's galley, I was looking out of the galley porthole in the waist of the ship near the butcher's shop, where the daily rum was issued. The hands were at dinner when suddenly the Royal Marine came into view. Looking about him in a furtive manner he went to the scupper and lifting the grating, he put down his hand and brought up a fanny, full of rum, the left overs from the daily grog issue which should have hit the sea.

'I had solved the mystery of the tiddly Marine! I cornered him as he was about to enter the butcher's shop with several tots in the fanny. After that it was an occasional piece of extra steak and — yes, you've guessed it! I was sorry when a few months later he blotted his copybook and was taken off Tanky's duties.'

Something very similar could happen on shore too. It did to Mr S N G Foulsham of Sunbury-on-Thames. *HMS Collingwood* was, at the time, a new entry training establishment at Fareham, near Portsmouth. 'My first electronics course completed at *HMS Collingwood*, I arrived at RN Barracks, Portsmouth, to await a draft to my first ship and was promptly made officer of the day's flunkey to help with the daily grog issue, still too young to draw my own ration. My task was to roll the brass-bound tub along the verandah at the top of the stone steps to where it received its lovingly measured mixture of rum and water.

'After the issue I was ordered to tip what must have been a quart of grog through the balustrade into the shrubbery below. I still don't know how I managed to hit the boiler-room pensioner's bald head, but the grog sprayed over his shoulders, completely missing the battered enamel teapot which he held up at shrub-top level. Only I could see him — or so I thought until I caught sight of the astonished face of the Royal Marine bugler who had followed me along the verandah. In thoughtful silence we took the tub back for inspection before stowing it.

'It wasn't too long before an aromatic and irate pensioner appeared in my caboose.
"You new on this job cocker? Didn't the other chap before you hand over to you properly?"
'I stuttered a respectful apology realising that the apparition before me had probably served in the navy years before finding this pensioner's dream of home. I explained that my predecessor had received a pier-head draft and went without our having met. He in his turn explained to me that he was *always* in the shrubbery at the crucial moment, and that the teapot would *always* be held in the same position for me to aim at. Our friendship blossomed, and I spent many a happy hour in a warm boiler room learning how to drink my tot like a man — "an wiv respeck".
'Alas we would have had more room and more grog if that Royal Marine bugler hadn't been a fly on the wall.'

The search for plushers occasionally went awry. In the following account an almost unbelievable sequence of events denied Mr P Habens of Cowes not only his entitlement to his daily tot, but to some well deserved plushers as well, 'Having joined the navy as a fifteen-year-old artificer apprentice I became accustomed to the smell of rum at an early age. I served the best part of five years under age, too young to receive the daily tot. However, "G" or Grog Day for me arrived on July 3, 1945, as a young killick. On my twentieth birthday I sailed through the Straits of Gibraltar en route for the far east onboard a troopship, the *Empress of Scotland*. She wore the red duster and not the white ensign of the RN. Sadly for me, such ships were dry.

'We disembarked at Colombo in Ceylon (now Sri Lanka). About ten miles south the navy had a transit camp amid a coconut plantation. Accommodation was in primitive huts called bandas — with no doors, and roofs made of woven palm leaves called cadgun. The important feature about this tropical paradise was the sign at the gate which read *HMS Serwa*, making it a ship within the meaning of the act. As such it enjoyed the midday pipe of Up Spirits.

'I filled in the customary request form, for permission to change from "UA" to "G", only to have my request rejected because my service documents had not arrived from England. In August the news broke; the war was over and Japan had surrendered. Them, came the order which settled the issue beyond doubt, Splice the main-brace. And I was still officially under age!

'On that fateful VJ Day, I happened to be duty leading hand required to stand by the rum tub and assist proceedings by seeing that no-one "went round the buoy" for a second issue. I stood inhaling the fumes of that elixir whilst everyone else contentedly drank their double ration. In the tub there remained the best part of a gallon.'

"Ditch it, Hookey" came the order from the officer of the day. I couldn't believe it!

' 'All of it, sir?" I asked.

' "Yes, all of it" came the curt reply.

'So came the final blow; I knew how the Japanese must have felt that day as I reverently tilted the tub on its side and watched the sandy soil thirstily swallow the last drop.'

In the battle to gain extra quantities of rum or grog, an element of dog eats dog invariably entered the proceedings.

Tanky, whose job it was to allocate grog to each mess from the tub, could by the skilful use of his thumb inside the measure, ensure a modest shortfall for his own eventual benefit — or so he hoped. The rum bos'n of the mess was not beyond employing a similar stratagem with his own messmates. It was often accepted by them, in fact, that whatever was left over, 'Queens' as it was known, was a fair reward for his pains. In the chiefs' and petty officers' messes, Queens was usually laid aside in a Come-in-handy-bottle which would be kept for moments of celebration or for offering to guests. The neat rum which they received held no storage problem.

An outstanding example of Queens' exploitation occurs in the experience of a young seaman at Devonport during the war. Let Mr P G Sellars tell it in his own words, 'In 1943, the RN Barracks were literally bursting at the seams with personnel awaiting a ship. My mess was a huge dormitory in charge of which were two old three-badge leading hands. Known as mess caterers it was their job to see that you turned to, kept things tidy, collected the mail, and of course drew the rum issue daily if entitled. The many hundreds crammed into the mess meant that as many as ten fannies of grog needed to be drawn so that on returning to the mess for one's tot it was not unusual to find a queue of thirty or forty waiting to reach the table where the old salts were dishing it out. One of the old badgers would first place his two forefingers (as thick as two pork sausages) inside the glass, scoop up the rum from the fanny, then pour it into the waiting cup. That would account for nearly a quarter of one's tot for a start, but en route the hand would be seized by jerks and spasms causing even more grog to slop back into the fanny. If anyone had the audacity to say, ''You're spilling my tot'', he would cast a bleary optic in one's direction, draw a deep breath and say, ''Listen young man, if you'd been on them Russian convoys like what I was — been dive-bombed, tin-fished, gone without sleep for days on end, battled your way to Murmansk and back again in freezing cold weather — and on hard tack, your b........ hand would shake a bit'', and everyone standing around would all nod their heads in accord.

'So after the issue and the hands had turned to for the afternoon, the old three-badgers would dutifully pour all the slops into big enamel jugs and spend the rest of the day with their cronies supping themselves into a happy state of modest inebriation, spinning yarns of bygone epics, and wait for the next day's issue to come round again.'

Sometimes the individual could do better than Queens if he brought inventiveness into play. Should an accident occur to a rum bos'n en route from the tub to his mess — which might happen quite genuinely in a force ten gale — he was entitled to ask the officer of the day for a replacement. A simple hard luck story was not enough — most OODs had heard them all before. It had to carry conviction with facts which could not be argued. Mr P F Foster of Portsmouth illustrates, 'As one of the three messmen allocated to the chief petty officers of HMS Tyne in 1958, I particularly enjoyed drawing the daily rum ration, savouring that sickly sweet smell which filled the spirit room flat and longing for the day when "UA" would be replaced by "G" in my pay book. It was fascinating to watch Jack Dusty skilfully juggle with the large copper measures as he poured the thirty-one tots into my rum fanny. Several decks above me, the chief shipwright was carrying out his own daily ritual. As soon as the boatswain's mate piped, Up Spirits, he would remove a chipped enamel mug from its hook above his bunk and hurry off to collect a sample of the soup of the day from the galley. Usually he would return to his office — which doubled as his cabin — and drink the soup. This day, however, he decided that conditions were right to carry out a pre-prepared plan.

'My route back to the mess took me past the chief shipwright's office. As I drew level with the door he ushered me quickly inside, picked up the enamel mug, and poured the contents into the rum. I stood there speechless watching the pale brown vegetable soup slowly spread across the surface of the rum.

' 'Right lad,'' he said, ''look seasick and worried.'' I needed no bidding — I *was* sick and worried. He almost frog-marched me back down to the spirit room where the tail end of the queue was still awaiting rum. Pushing to the front he held out my arm so that the offending mixture of rum and soup was clearly visible to the supervising officer.

' ''The messman has been sick in the rum, sir,'' he informed the lieutenant. ''Take it away and ditch it. We'll give you another issue,'' said the officer, recoiling from the revolting sight.

'Later that night after the mixture had been carefully strained through a cheese cloth, I and two fellow messmen enjoyed our first ever full tot of neaters in the shipwright's caboose.'

A rum barricoe (or breaker) and rum tub set against the appropriate background of HMS Victory

One further example from Mr D R Thorne of Bath shows the importance of rum recovery, 'We had gathered in the mess about 11am waiting for the highlight of the day — the arrival of Tanky and his fanny of rum. Eventually his footsteps were heard on the iron deck above, and then the clank from the fanny against the hatch as he started his perilous way down. Suddenly there was a despairing yell, followed immediately by a loud metallic clatter. The effect on the mess was electrifying; immediately there was a rush on the tiny mess flat to see our worst fears confirmed — the fanny lying on the deck and Tanky curled in a corner, groaning.

'There was no time to waste — instantly and collectively we sized up the problem. To our eternal shame we ignored the wounded Tanky — who obviously was not about to expire judging by his language — and desperately grabbed anything available to save what we could before the ship's pitching and rolling dispatched our life blood into inaccessible places. We were only too well aware that the adjacent mess across the flat was taking an unhealthy interest in events and might offer to help.

'In a short time we were able to give aid and comfort to the indignant Tanky and the salvaged spirit was placed in a bottle for later straining to remove foreign matter. Needless to say, the officer of the day was deeply suspicious when we asked for rum replacement but it would have requird a hard-hearted man to ignore Tanky's twisted ankle and bruises. It was given us; Tanky recovered with dramatic speed, and we all helped him to splice the main-brace.'

Lukewarm rum was never popular, and so it was that in hot and humid climates, ice was a useful addition which many messes employed. A cunning device by the occasional rum bos'n, not too troubled by moral scruples, was to add ice to the grog fanny immediately after issue so that by the time the mess-deck was reached it had dissolved. In senior messes ice was sometimes added to the neat tot even in temperate climes. One chief petty officer when asked by the young and innocent mess-man why he did so was told, 'Because I like to see it grow lad, I like to see it grow.'

'In a submarine, HMS Alliance, in the early 1960s, the number of her crew entitled to daily rum was sixty-four which, by a remarkable coincidence, was exactly the number of tots contained in a one-gallon stoneware rum jar,' writes Mr G Marshall of Sittingbourne. 'The boat had not been at diving stations for a week, the atmosphere inside was most unpleasant, and both temperature and humidity were extremely high. The daily spirit ration, although eagerly anticipated, was not appreciated in the normal way as it was too warm and fiery. The addition of ice cubes had been tried but the senior rates did not like the dilution of their neat rum.

'The crew hit upon the idea of putting the sealed gallon of rum in the deep freeze the day before issue. The next day the seal on the jar was broken and the coxswain began to issue rum but when it came to the last mess issue for the chief and petty officers ten tots were required, whereas only just over nine tots remained. The mess generously agreed to make up the deficiency from their plushers bottle.

'On the following day the same ritual was followed but despite a sparing issue by the coxswain, the senior rates mess was again short. Consternation grew. On the third day a thorough check was carried out on all measurements but again the jar was short. The senior rates plushers bottle was now almost empty and an explanation had to be found. An unopened jar was taken from the spirit room, carefully measured and found to contain the exact imperial gallon. On the fourth day this jar was used but again was found wanting.

'At last the penny dropped. A gallon of rum contracts in volume by almost one tot after being kept in the deep freeze for twenty-four hours. The moral of course was to allow one tot of water to every jar of rum before issue to allow for any eventuality such as spillage or shrinkage. This cooled rum proved to be a delight to drink and was smooth and pleasant, according to the connoisseurs!'

Reference has been made to the ancient device known as 'bulling' whereby an empty cask could be made to render one last offering. Mr E. Attwood, now eighty-one years of age can remember that when he was serving in HMS *Whitshed* in 1920, the coxswain in company with the officer of the day, would open the spirit room every Thursday morning, and bring up a cask of rum which would be decanted into one-gallon wicker jars. These were locked in store, and the empty cask placed behind the ladder in the flat until the following Thursday when the spirit room was again opened.

As soon as the coxswain was gone, one man would remove the bung, pour in a jug of boiling water, and roll the cask backwards and forwards. The rolling action would be repeated every time a messmate passed the cask on his way to the mess.

Twenty-four hours later the contents were removed. The boiling water had drawn the remaining rum from the wood, to provide a strong nightcap of pusser's. The crew got away with this for about eighteen months, until the coxswain found out. One night their extra tot, much to their disgust, was full of salt, and that was that.'

The temptation to take rum ashore was also great. The degree of any crime varied from the limited attainment of taking a ration ashore for consumption in homely surroundings, to the other extreme of obtaining rum illicitly for removal in bulk from the ship.

In May 1948, writes Lieutenant (E) D W Edwards RN (retired), the Second Flotilla of Motor Torpedo Boats put into the Cornish harbour of Fowey where the boats moored in trots in midstream. The home of the petty officer motor mechanic of one of the boats was nearby, and he was granted all night leave. Waiting in uniform, at a bus stop ashore, the petty officer was approached by a customs officer who asked to see inside the small case he was carrying. Not wishing to be searched in public and aware of his rights, the petty officer asked that this should be in private, whereupon the two returned to the customs house. Here the petty officer was momentarily left on his own in the office whereupon he removed the bottle of rum he had in his case and flung it out of the window. The building, typical of an old west country seaport, stood at water's edge. The window overlooked the harbour and the discarded bottle fell into it. News of the event soon spread through the boats. At the next low tide a swarm of matelots, with trousers rolled up, were paddling around in the shallows, all with eyes down! No-one ashore seemed to understand what it was all about except perhaps that frustrated customs officer!'

The best laid schemes o' mice and men, gang aft a-gley, and certainly the plan in this story from Mr Don Lydon of Dublin deserved its fate, 'In March 1960, I served in *HMS Adamant* on the Gareloch at Faslane. As petty officers' messman it was my duty to collect their rum ration daily. Being partial to "neaters" but entitled to grog, and not finding the president of the mess

(Left) A typical pump used for siphoning rum from the cask in the spirit room (right) Typical lip-type measures for issuing neaters

generous in that direction, I hatched a plan that would net me a tot daily. All I required was a small funnel, two miniature spirit bottles — one empty and one filled with water — and, of course, a steady hand. The plan was that en route from the rum store, I would fill the empty bottle with rum and decant the other of water into the rum fanny. It worked so well that soon I was drawing off two tots daily with never a complaint from the petty officers about the quality of the tot. In fact I found it hard at times to keep a straight face watching them smacking their lips as they downed their "neaters". Little did they know.

'A week before annual leave I started bottling my illicit gains to surprise an old friend who had served in the RN and to whom the tot was just a happy memory. I duly filled a large wine bottle and hid it in my hold-all. Armed with leave pass, I approached the main gate knowing the risk I was running and uttering a silent prayer that I should not be searched. None other than the mess president was on duty at the gate.

' "I'll be all right here," I thought to myself.

' "Hello, Mick," he exclaimed, "going on a spot of leave?"

'He glanced at my pass and gave me the nod to carry on. I breathed a sigh of relief, but too soon; just as I was leaving the hut he called me back.

' "Let's have a look in the hold-all."

'My heart missed a beat or two as I unzipped it and he began the search. Slowly his hands emerged clutching my precious

bottle festooned with underwear.

' "This is it," I thought as I saw my leave vanishing to be replaced with barred windows.

'"What's this, what's this?" he exclaimed holding the prize aloft. He uncapped the bottle, sniffed the contents, winked at me, replaced the cap, and put it back in my hold-all.

' "Have a good leave Mick, and easy on that stuff."

'With those words he sent me on my way. I detected a faint smile as I beat a hasty retreat and boarded the bus for Helensburgh.

' "What a good guy," I thought slowly recovering from my ordeal.

'Comfortably seated on the train for Glasgow I decided a good gulp from the bottle would be just what the doctor ordered. With shaking hands I raised it to my lips and took a good long draught. Too late I realised my mistake. I have a terrible feeling that what the bottle contained was man-made and it certainly wasn't for drinking. No wonder the mess president was smiling.'

Sippers, gulpers, etc, came within the category of clean, innocent fun in contrast to the carefully prepared plans for wholesale rum gains which were engineered from time to time. It stands to reason that the two people so deeply involved in the daily rum issue — Jack Dusty and Tanky — were the most vulnerable to temptation and wrongdoing. Tanky in particular, who performed the actual handling, not to mention the drinking — for most Tankies were 'G' to a man — needed to be of strong character. Apart from anything else, it was Tanky's task to use all the implements for issuing rum, and these could be turned to his advantage. Dented measures, misuse of the dipping stick when taking cask readings, and trapping rum in the pump could all be exploited. Even the withdrawal of small amounts of rum from the spirit room by substituting water was not unknown as an account from Mr W Mortimer of Southsea shows, 'In the mid 1930's I was serving onboard HMS *Iron Duke*. My job was after flat sweeper with yards and yards of corticene to polish plus the brasswork. The after flat possessed a hatch leading to the spirit room. Every day before eleven, a three-badge Tanky would arrive to unclip the hatch. Tanky's job involved bringing along all the rum measures, opening the hatch, going down the ladder, and waiting outside the locked spirit room for the duty warrant officer and representatives from senior messes to arrive. The rum was then measured out and passed back up top.

'This particular morning I was by the hatch when Tanky arrived a little late. Flinging back the hatch he started to dive below when, one of the supposed empty rum measures caught on the combing of the hatch and out shot a stream of water. There was dead silence as Tanky's face paled.

' "Don't say anything," he croaked.

' "I'm not getting involved, but I'll mop up quickly before the gang arrive," I replied.

'That was fifty years ago, but I have often thought back and wondered how many were in the swindle. After all Tanky could hardly have scrubbed out the spirit room with a rum measure of cold water!'

It would be quite unfair to represent Tanky as the accepted villain in the piece. Skulduggery was not his monopoly by a long way. The following story from Mr Carl Hayman of Worcester serves to show that the opportunity was open to many — frequently without success, 'The Gunner of our wartime destroyer seemed untroubled by any of the usual hazards that the Battle of the Atlantic produced; a cheerful soul, he presided over the daily rum issue like a merry high priest. And like a high priest, he accepted libations of rum from various members of the ship's company. But, the like the famed Oliver Twist, he always wanted more.

'The year 1941 produced a nasty crop of U-boats, and Guns (as he was known) was in his element urging our depth charge crews to greater efforts, as we swept into yet another attack. A shallow pattern of depth charges malfunctioned with a near surface burst, shattering quite a lot of stuff aft. Drawing the jars of rum afterwards, Guns was overjoyed to discover several of them smashed, but still containing a fair quantity of his favourite tipple; which, at the speed of light, he transferred to old whisky bottles, and prepared the necessary paperwork for three jars of rum to be written off.

'After our return to Liverpool Guns soon ran out of the where-withal for his favourite drink and seemed glad when we cleared Gladstone Dock to join an outward bound convoy. As we headed west the sea was calm and even more surprisingly U-boats seemed to be conspicuous by their absence. We reached mid-Atlantic, picked up our homeward bound convoy, and headed once again for the Western Approaches. The nearer we got to land, the more unhappy Guns became. Once or twice he was seen lurking by the depth charge racks aft, apparently either praying or cursing. We thought it strange, especially as we were all looking forward to a long leave resulting from an overdue boiler clean and refit.

'Suddenly Guns was drafted out of the ship. It wasn't until several weeks later, that our usual tight-lipped coxswain gave us the reason for Guns' rapid departure. Apparently he had decided to broach a jar or two of bubbly by cracking them with a well-placed hammer and then happily write them off as lost by enemy action as before. Unfortunately for him Hitler provided no action that trip, leaving Guns with a lot of explaining to do. Which he couldn't, and didn't.'

A sail on our lee-bow appears
    She looms like a French Man-of-War
Then pipe up all hands, my brave Tars
    And cheerly for chasing prepare . . .

But now see her topsails aback
    She seems making ready to fight
Up hammocks! down chests!
    clear the deck!
And see all your matches alight

Now splice the main-brace
    and to quarters away!

Naval Chronicle 1805

CHAPTER ELEVEN

Pot pourri

IMMEDIATE
From: C in C Mediterranean
To: Mediterranean Station
HM The King directs me to convey to all concerned his appreciation of the efficiency and appearance of the allied ships and establishments and their companies which he saw in Italian waters.

Time of origin 030934 Aug

IMMEDIATE
From: C in C Mediterranean
To: Mediterranean Station
Splice the main-brace   Time of origin 030936 Aug

It was in such manner that the welcome news of an additional tot of rum was conveyed to officers and men serving in recent times. It was — and still is with minor modification — the privilege of royalty and of Admiralty to order 'splice the main-brace'. The occasions have always been rare but it has been said that by sheer instinct most matelots knew when they were about to be favoured and that many knew the flag signal by heart.

As so often with a naval custom, the origin of the expression 'splice the main-brace' is difficult to trace; indeed it has been said that the main-brace had no splice and that the use of the term is a fallacy. Up to a point the assessment is correct but the true answer is discernible by analysing the few available historical references. The first use of the expression was made in the

Napoleonic wars, the ballad opening this chapter providing one such example.

Another appears in the memoirs of Admiral Dillon. When in 1794 *HMS Defence* in which he served as a midshipman had a narrow escape from being wrecked, Dillon commented, 'It was the custom in all cases of extra exertion at sea to give the seamen a dram apiece, which was called Splicing the mainbrace.'

The interesting point, apart from the use of the expression itself, is that in neither instance is the physical act of splicing the main-brace connected with the reason for giving the men additional rum. In the one case the intention was to instil 'Dutch courage' before a battle and, in the other, as a means of rewarding efforts in preserving the ship from disaster.

Further proof of the corruption of the expression appears in the experiences of C R Pemberton who as a boy ran away from home. He and another young lad found themselves being followed by members of the 'press' in the streets of Liverpool in 1807, and they submitted to the gang's gentle persuasion which took the following form '. . . our ship is a gallows deal finer than any you've seen yet, and with a jolly good captain too; he splices the main-brace every week, and every time of close-reef topsails.'

It should be explained that the main-brace — dating back to the early days of sail — had performed the vital function of controlling the main yard with its heavy course of canvas. There were two braces to each yard fastened diagonally to allow it to be slewed to port or starboard. Should a main-brace part, the ship had to remain on the same tack until replacement or repair had been completed.

It is certainly true that the main-brace as fitted when new was not spliced, but every item of rigging had an understandable habit of wearing out — usually at an inconvenient moment when a gale was blowing. If the cordage required to replace the main-brace was unavailable, the only recourse in emergency with the safety of the ship probably in the balance was to splice using the most experienced seamen under the boatswain's supervision. It was an exacting task demanding speed, resilience and professional knowledge, and an exercise for which a small reward was entirely justified.

In the beginning, the award of extra rum for splicing the main-brace was for that specific act. Later, and certainly by

Nelson's time, the reward had been extended to other acts calling for endurance in their execution. Finally, the extra rum provided an opportunity for the reigning monarch or the Admiralty to bestow their approval on an outstanding event or for a special celebration. After King George III had visited the navy at Portsmouth in 1789 a double allowance of rum instead of the day's beer ration was issued by his order. Again by the King's order a similar reward was made in 1794 after Admiral Howe's victory at the battle of the Glorious First of June.

Today, the expression is interpreted more widely and is used as a casual invitation to a celebration party. In short, 'let's splice the main-brace' is akin to 'let's have a drink'.

Fleet reviews have usually been fitting occasions for splicing the main-brace, but the royal dispensation has also been used at less commonplace moments. In 1947, King George VI took passage in *HMS Vanguard* — the last battleship to be built for the Royal Navy — for a tour of South Africa. In the early forenoon of February 10, the ship's position was latitude 00° 00', longitude 09° 30'W, and the Crossing the Line ceremony was about to begin.

Falconer's eighteenth century *Marine Dictionary* gives this version of the event thus, 'All persons solicitous of purchasing their freedom of Old Neptune bribe the superintendents of the ceremony with a gallon of rum and a few pounds of sugar; but if they neglect to do this they must expect to go through with the whole operation.'

At exactly 0900, the ceremony onboard the *Vanguard* began with the arrival of the 'Royal Trumpeters' followed by the police, in preparation for the inspection of the Royal Guard. King Neptune and Queen Amphitrite were then welcomed by the Commander, who led them to inspect the Guard — all bootnecks (Royal Marines) in disguise. The guard and band marched off leading the whole assembly to the stage and huge canvas bath rigged abreast of "A" turret on the starboard side. The Clerk of the Court then announced, "My Lords, Ladies and Gentlemen, the Court of His Most Turbulent Majesty, King Neptune is now in session." The Captain escorted the Royal Family to the scene of the proceedings. Before reaching the stage, His Majesty observed a stranded twenty-four inch manilla rope lying on the deck

His Majesty Captain, what have we here? It's in a sorry plight.

Captain Sir, that's the main-brace.
His Majesty Then have it spliced.
Captain Aye aye, sir (and to the boatswain
conveniently standing by), splice the main-brace.

The boatswain piped and passed the word to splice the main-brace to the accompaniment of loud cheering from the onlookers. The Captain then mounted the platform with the Royal Family who took their seats. When the royal introductions to King Neptune had been made and the "Crossing the line" certificates presented, the general hunt ensued for victims to suffer at the hands of Neptune's acolytes. No-one escaped, not even Neptune, Amphitrite, and their retinue, all of whom were left floundering in the water.'

Prince Charles, born the following year in 1948, had an early and unusual connection with splicing the main-brace. Mr F Robson of Pinner explains, 'I recall with nostalgia a Royal celebration which resulted in my being issued with not one, two or three, but four official tots of the finest pusser's rum. It happened on the day the Prince of Wales was born — November 14, when his mother was still Princess Elizabeth. I was serving in *HMS Mull of Kintyre*, a liberty-type ship moored near Rothesay Bay, in the Firth of Clyde. Part of the crew and some scientists serving with the ship were concerned with experiments being carried out on a number of veteran wartime ships higher up the loch in a quiet backwater shielded by steep-sided hills. Here they were subjected to the blast of explosives and other indignities.

'I had been detailed to work off the ship on that particular day in company with the boffins. On returning close to teatime, the number of hammocks slung in the messdeck signalled that there had been a make-and-mend. A face appearing over the side of a hammock lost no time in goading me for having worked while others slumbered. "Princess Elizabeth has had a son and heir, and we've all had an extra tot", and, after a pause, "we've sunk yours as well". The leading hand of the mess deciding that the joke had gone far enough explained, "We spliced the main-brace and yours is here — two instead of one."

'As I was about to take my first sip, the master-at-arms appeared and enquired whether the grog had gone flat as it had been mixed four hours earlier. Feeling that a little play acting was required, I told the master that I had never kept a tot waiting four minutes, let alone four hours. The face of the master-of-arms — a strict man but always fair — remained impassive.

'"If your grog is flat then tell me," he thundered. I gave it a further test expanding on the previous sip to a complete swallow.

' "I think it's flat, master," I managed to say.

' "Right, lad," he broke in, "if your tot is flat, in accordance with the regulations you will have another, but as we have spliced the main-brace, you will have another two if that is what you want."

'One of my golden rules during my time afloat was never to go against what the master-at-arms said. The rum bos'n was summoned, and two more tots were produced. The birthday treat improved by the minute. I can't remember how long I took to sink my third and fourth tots that November evening, but the glow lasted for days.

'Perhaps one day the Prince will learn how his birthday contributed to making November 14, 1948 the happiest day I spent in his grandfather's Navy.' ·

Happily this age-old custom survives to maintain its link with the past even though the rum ration ceased in 1970. All officers and ratings over the age of eighteen are still entitled to an eighth of a pint of spirits — or two cans of beer if spirits are unavailable — whenever splice the main-brace is ordered. Her Majesty's silver jubilee in 1976 provided just such an occasion. The flag signal hoisted for splice the main-brace has varied at different periods as shown in the diagrams on page 151.

Christmas Day was another occasion in the navy when rum used to flow. Contrary to regulations men saved their rum beforehand with the result that in the early days of the issue it was unsafe for officers to visit the seamen's messes. In the last hundred years or so, the day has still been celebrated with the flowing bowl and much merriment, but it has also provided the opportunity for a get-together of officers and men to everyone's benefit. Captains of ships usually tour the messes on Christmas morning, and the lighthearted inspection is frequently enlivened by an exchange of uniforms, with for example, a junior rating appearing as the master-at-arms and other similar inversions of normal relationships, a custom that is said to have been practised as far back as Roman times. Today, rum no longer makes its contribution to Christmas but the tradition of decorating the mess to make it feel as much like home as possible is as strong as ever.

Ballads, dancing, toasting and leg pulling, each in their way have helped to form the character of the seaman and are part of his heritage. They have their origins in a need for self-entertainment when men could forget their hard and isolated shipboard life. Grog was usually close at hand,

> And now arrived that jovial night,
> When every true bred Tar carouses;
> When o'er the grog all hands delight
> To toast their sweethearts and their spouses.
>
> Round went the can, the jest, the glee,
> While tender wishes fill'd each fancy,
> And when in turn it came to me,
> I heaved a sigh, and toasted Nancy.

The 'jovial night' was celebrated on Saturday when the traditional toast was, 'Sweethearts and wives', and the response in officers' messes was 'and may they never meet'. The seaman also had to enjoy most of his carousing in the shoreside tavern but his repertoire of songs and ballads seemed never ending with titles such as, 'The lass that loves a sailor', 'The heart that can feel for another', 'Those we left behind us', 'The sailor's sweetheart', 'What will you do love?' and many others.

In those days when there was an evening issue of grog onboard, the habit of toasting was more widespread. 'Sweethearts and wives' remained inseparable from Saturday, but there were other secondary toasts which were honoured on other days of the week. The custom was: Sunday, absent friends; Monday, our ships at sea; Tuesday, our men; Wednesday, ourselves; Thursday, bloody war and quick promotion, or The King; Friday, A willing foe and plenty of sea room.

A toast drunk less regularly was that on the occasion of a ship's

Take your partners. Not much
choice for sailors aboard
HMS Donegal at the turn of the century

return from abroad. The custom took the form of removing particles of sand and grit adhering to the tallow when soundings were taken with the lead, and dropping these into the grog tub, and then toasting, 'Happiness and prosperity to our native land'. Sightings of land were also toasted or rewarded in the earlier days of sail. Captain James Cook's log in the *Endeavour* reveals that when the ship was approaching the coast of New Zealand in 1769 a gallon of rum was promised to the member of the crew who should first sight land so that he could toast the event and, incidentally, have the land named after him. Disconcertingly, the prize was won by a sharp-sighted boy of twelve, borne as a supernumerary, Nicholas Youngs by name. 'Young Nick's Head' features on the chart or map today, but it must be assumed that the toasting in rum must have been shared by his adult shipmates.

For many years it has been the custom in officers' messes to drink the loyal toast seated, a privilege which is believed to have originated with Charles II's return to England from Holland in 1660 when he had the misfortune to bump his head on an overhead beam when rising to reply to a toast. There are many other explanations but by royal dispensation the privilege is still

granted. In 1964, it was extended by Queen Elizabeth to officers and non-commissioned officers of the Royal Marines and later, in 1966, to chief and petty officers of the Royal Navy when dining formally in their messes.

Celebration in many forms continues to play an important part of naval life despite the absence of grog. Even such an event as celebrating the Siege of Gibraltar is still taken as an excuse for a tot of spirits if not of grog, in the same way that a single green and white pennant (popularly known as the Gin Pennant) at the

Even muzzle-loaders could not spoil the Christmas festivities aboard the ironclad HMS Achilles in 1875

hoist indicates to officers in other ships that there is an invitation to come and join the party.

Dancing in all-male company may sound odd but in the navy it has always been regarded as an effective way of taking exercise in cramped surroundings. The solo jig and hornpipe of earlier days was slowly overtaken by the *pas de deux* of the Victorian navy when seamen danced together in bare feet, frequently with clay pipes jutting from their mouths. The fiddler playing the accompaniment also gave way to the ship's band of later years. Such dancing was encouraged by authority, but perhaps over zealously by Captain Bligh, whose log contains this entry on a day when the *Bounty* was in the tropics, 'Two men discovered to be shirking their evening dancing had their grog stopped . . . for risking their health.'

The art of 'taking the mickey' — the navy's favourite expression for a leg pull — has always been highly developed, and many victims have been found from the ranks of the newly joined. When rum features so much in daily life, it was often used as an excuse for fun as this wartime account by Mr N Lee of Trowbridge shows, 'I joined the cruiser *HMS Dunedin* direct from training on December 8, 1939. The commanding officer was Captain (later Admiral of the Fleet) Charles Lambe. About the end of January 1940 we went on Icelandic patrol. It was the first time I had ever been to sea and it was very rough and freezing cold. Moreover, my cruising station as a member of number two six-inch gun's crew was very exposed, and we would shelter as best we could behind the captain's sea cabin. On this particular day the rum issue was late, and we had closed up at the gun for the afternoon watch before those entitled had received their tot. I was under twenty and did not qualify but one of our messmates brought the rum rations to the others a little later.

'I was standing shivering in the icy spray when one of the crew said, "Here you are, this'll warm you", handing me his cup containing over half a tot. I thanked him, drank it down and handed him back the cup.

' "I didn't mean you to drink the flaming tot," he glowered. I had never drunk alcohol in my life and a warm glow with other after effects quickly overcame me and the others must have known instantly that I was fair game.

'Said one, "If your hands are cold you can have the pair of gloves I loaned the skipper the other day when I was on the bridge if you care to ask him for them", for which I thanked him saying that I would ask the captain next time he came down from the bridge, not realising that he was taking the mickey.

'Shortly afterwards, the captain came below to go to his sea cabin. As I approached him the remainder beat a hasty retreat. I was left on my own but, fortified by the rum, I said to the captain, "Excuse me, sir, Able Seaman Wainwright said I could have the gloves he lent you the other day." The captain, being a kindly man, first asked my name and then smiled.

' "He's pulling your leg, son." He went into his cabin while the gun's crew came out of their hiding places laughing their heads off. I felt dreadful.

Suddenly my name was called and it was the captain once again.

' "Here you are, Lee, it's your turn to laugh now." Thanking him profusely I turned round and returned to the gun's crew. You should have seen their faces for the captain had given me a lovely pair of thick knitted mittens.'

'Taking the mickey' could achieve more sophisticated heights. Officers and petty officers shared in it, shown by this post-war event described by Mr D. Cranwell of Fawley, Hampshire.

'While serving in the submarine depot ship *HMS Montclare* at Rothesay in 1948, I became involved in a dispute about physical strength of two petty officer friends, Tiffy, well known for accepting mess-deck challenges such as press-ups and arm wrestling, and Blackie, the ship's blacksmith nearing the end of his career, but still strong in the arm.

'One day the latter casually mentioned (in a loud voice!) that he daily exercised with a bar-bell which he thought might be too heavy for any of those present to lift. In fact, he was willing to bet his tot that the bar couldn't be "clean jerked". It was a foregone conclusion that someone would challenge his claim. Tiffy was that someone, upping the challenge to a week's tot. Blackie reluctantly agreed.

'A few days later a number of petty officers gathered in the foundry where Blackie could be seen dressed in his usual overalls and sweat rag, and Tiffy, the centre of attraction in his singlet, shorts and gym shoes. The Physical Training Instructor, acting as referee, whipped away the canvas covering with a touch of showmanship and Tiffy, amid cheers and jeers, bent to his task. Firmly grasping the bar, he gave an almighty heave and nearly ruptured himself for life! Blackie had spot-welded the bar to the deck.'

'All sale, loan, transfer, gift or barter of spirit whatsoever, is prohibited.' So read the naval regulations on rum in early Victorian days but because such an edict was palpably impossible to enforce it was observed with a nod and a wink. Minor trading in rum was at most times recognised as a socially acceptable tradition of naval life provided it was kept within bounds but the attitude towards wholesale trafficking was viewed in a more serious light. Those caught indulging in it deserved the retribution meted out to them.

When the initial trifling quarterly addition to pay was given to those electing not to draw their grog, the majority decided there was little to be gained from it. Greater benefit could be derived by trading in the ration for a variety of services rendered — by the ship's tailor, for example. Later, when life became more sophisticated and the monetary allowance more realistic, the emphasis changed from trading to handing over grog in exchange for a favour such as standing in for a duty.

The etiquette became well defined in the 1939-45 war when new entrants into the navy instituted their own version of the tot barter which remained until abolition. Sippers was a gentlemanly sip from a friend's rum issue when proferred. Gulpers — one big swallow from another's tot (but only one!). Sandy Bottoms — a rare gift — meant drinking the whole contents of the glass. Many regulars looked with disdain upon these variations of the long-established practice which had the merit, however, of acting as a safety valve. Provided an individual was not given an overdose of gulpers from his well-intentioned friends — which happened from time to time — it was probably the best system for maintaining an unofficial control.

In earlier times, rum's acceptance as a means of payment for goods or services was more evident ashore than afloat. Admiral Knowles, in his despatches to England after the capture of Louisbourg in 1746, mentioned that the New Englanders 'would gladly subsist us wholly with rum would I but suffer them', meaning, of course, that rum was currency to the New Englanders of North America.

Rum acquired an even higher value in the New South Wales colony which was founded in 1788 as a penal settlement to ease overcrowding in English jails. It took four years for the colony to become self-supporting and food supplies from England were iregular and meagre. But one sizeable import for which there was an insatiable demand from the mixed bag of convicts, sailors, public servants, garrison troops and later, free settlers, was rum. It all started with the New South Wales Corps, the Rum Battalion as it was colloquially known, which dominated colonial affairs. The corps had been raised by special recruiting when convict transportation began, and possessed no tradition or military honours. In the main its members were roughnecks who claimed the monopoly of all rum coming into the colony, and because there was so little ordinary money in circulation, rum quickly became an accepted form of currency. In the hands of this unscrupulous minority it acquired a value which encouraged graft and corruption. It was in his attempt to remedy this state of affairs that Captain Bligh, when colonial governor in 1806, faced yet another crisis in his turbulent career.

The old tar of a bygone era when asked what he thought of his daily rum said that it was, 'akin to drinking a fireball whose glowing warmth could soon be felt spreading hot and tingly from my stomach to the outer extremities of nearly frozen fingers, and a short time later I felt like living again'.

Maybe so but the principle if carried too far had disastrous consequences and the influence of rum in promoting mutiny provides one of the sadder reflections. The mutiny on board the frigate *Hermione* in 1797, resulting in the death or throwing overboard of the captain and most of the officers, was a bloody business, the stain of which was only partly erased by the eventual capture of the ringleaders. The main causes were an unpopular and callous captain and smouldering rebellion fanned by events in France. It would therefore be unfair to ascribe all blame to the demon rum, but the fact remains that mutiny broke out after the group of men had slaked their thirst from a bucket of rum on the forecastle.

Many more witnesses for the prosecution could be provided to give evidence against rum — the accused — but at least an equal number would be prepared to speak in its defence. No tribunal is necessary to arrive at a balanced judgement. Rum has gone from the navy but justice requires that the balance should be restored by one or two stories in its support.

In introducing this story from Mr J N Thwaite of Wantage it should be said that the *HMS Edinburgh* referred to, is the self-same ship from which a fortune in gold was recovered in 1981,

'In 1942, *HMS Edinburgh* wearing the flag of Vice-Admiral Bonham-Carter was on Russian convoy duty and I was serving as an ordinary signalman. We had escorted a convoy to Kola Inlet in North Russia and were returning as escort to convoy QP12. At 1530 on April 30, some 200 miles north of Murmansk in the Barents Sea, we were torpedoed twice by a German submarine. One torpedo blew fifty foot off the stern and the other hit the starboard side. I was in the signalmen's mess at the time and proceeded to my action station position on the flag deck. The upper deck was a shambles and many shipmates had been killed and wounded. With only one screw turning the ship managed to keep underway until we were joined by two destroyers, the *Foresight* and the *Forester*, and two Russian destroyers. Bulkheads were shored up by the damage control parties and the wounded were taken to a temporary hospital set up in the wardroom. On the flag deck the weather was cold with heavy snow squalls. We began a painful four knots back to Murmansk.

'Early next morning the Russian destroyers left us and were replaced by three minesweepers. Our galleys were out of action but the cooks worked miracles in providing hot drinks, soup and sandwiches to keep us going. All that night we could hear the bulkheads creaking under sea pressure with an occasional deeper rumble as a bulkhead collapsed; but we had great faith in our ship. About 0730 in the morning of May 2, three large German destroyers appeared and were engaged by our two much smaller destroyers. Although receiving heavy punishment they succeeded in sinking one and driving off another. The *Edinburgh* with only one turret operational engaged the third German destroyer and managed to hit it, but not before it had fired its torpedoes. The ship was struck on the port side this time and broke almost in two.

One of the minesweepers risking the very real danger of the cruiser capsizing, came alongside our port side to take off the remainder of our ship's company. HMS *Edinburgh*, by then a floating hulk, was despatched by a torpedo from one of our own ships. Once aboard the minesweeper the shock and reaction of the preceding forty hours set in so that when the pipe came for all survivors to muster for a tot of rum I was hardly able to stand. I was only eighteen and therefore unentitled to rum. Hoping that I would not draw attention to myself by my miserable state, I joined the queue. I was noticed by one of the regulating staff who would have turned me away had it not been for the master-at-arms who spoke sharply saying all survivors were to be given a tot of rum adding to me,

' "Come on, lad, drink up. It will do you the world of good."

'I had had the odd sippers and gulpers from messmates previously, but never a whole tot to myself before. It warmed the cockles of my heart and gone was the fear and trembling. Dutch courage perhaps, but we could even laugh and joke about our situation. That taste of pusser's rum will stay in my mind for just about the rest of my life.'

In the spring of 1943, the war against the U-boats in the Atlantic was at its height and the British success rate was improving rapidly. Here is a brief account by Mr Harry Newson of London, SE26, of one action in which the honours were shared, but showing once again the value of rum: 'Imagine the scene — the torpedomen's mess deck aboard HMS *Harvester* on March 11, 1943, the morning after we had rammed U-444 in the North Atlantic. The U-boat had become wedged under our stern for an agonising ten minutes and, when she eventually broke free, an explosion crippled one of our engines. Knowing that we could only make about ten knots, we accepted the inevitable fate of our ship — at the mercy of another member of the wolf pack.

'The pusser's tot was brought to our mess deck earlier than usual, and only two of us had been served when we heard and felt the explosion that meant the end of our ship. My messmates had scrambled up the ladder to go on deck when, glancing round, I spotted the jug of rum. Thinking, "That's too good to waste, and if I'm going to swim I might as well be prepared", I downed the rest in one great gulp! When the command came, "Every man for himself" as the ship began to break up, I went into the icy sea well fortified by my unexpectedly large tot. It saved my bacon.'

It is apt that the valedictory should be given by a senior rating Mr R Parker of North Cheam, Surrey who served for many years in the Royal Navy. This is his verdict, 'Most ex-regulars — I dislike the term Old Salts which seems more applicable to the days of wooden ships — have fond memories of pusser's rum and find it hard to imagine a Royal Navy without it. The tot had many advantages. It could open doors (sometimes gates), bolster friendships, heal rifts, facilitate dockyard deals (and even speed up refits), oil many a wheel, act as a morale booster, give Dutch courage in the thick of battle — and to landing parties, help cure colds and other ills of the body and mind, and speed many a parting old shipmate to his new destination.

'It could also unfortunately become dangerous if taken to excess, as in the case — many will recall — of twin seaman boys who sadly died as the result of too many sippers on their sixteenth birthday. I had a bitter-sweet experience myself of such an excess when in 1941 I left my ship in Port Said shortly after a Malta convoy. I was due to leave after tot time that particular morning. Sippers came from all and sundry and I was out for the rest of the day. From then on until the end of my service days twelve years later, it was definitely a case of one man, one tot, and I valued it on that basis.'

Who better than that enigmatic character Captain Bligh to bring down the curtain? When he had lost control of the situation in *HMS Bounty* and the mutineers had gained the upper hand, most showed signs of heavy drinking. Their immoderation made them violent and insistent that Bligh should be cast adrift in the launch with his seventeen companions. About three gallons of rum were passed into the boat, perhaps as a salve to their consciences. Bligh allocated a daily ration of a teaspoonful of rum per man on his epic voyage to safety across the Pacific Ocean and it probably saved their lives. There is no better example than this to illustrate the importance of the good and the bad of rum on those men who through the centuries were the prime part of Britain's walls of oak — the Royal Navy.

Once cast adrift the survival of Captain Bligh and loyal members of his crew without a small daily allowance of rum would have been hazarded

Appendices

APPENDIX I

Memorandum as to the manner in which rum is purchased for the use of the Royal Navy, and its subsequent treatment

Rum is purchased for the use of the Navy through the Admiralty Brokers, Messrs E and F Man.

When purchased, it is about 40 per cent over proof.

Before Rum thus purchased is removed from the bonded warehouse in the docks to Deptford Yard it is 're-examined' by the Customs authorities in order to ascertain the *actual contents* as compared with the 'landing account' *ie,* the contents when the Rum was originally landed from the ship and taken into bond.

On arrival at the Yard, the actual contents of each puncheon are again ascertained by the Yard officers by dipping with a gauging rod, and the strength is taken by Sikes' Hydrometer. The quantity thus ascertained is then calculated out to proof strength, compared with the Customs despatch, and, if found correct, taken on charge as so many gallons of proof spirit.

The method of calculating strong Rum to proof strength is to multiply the ullage (which in this sense means the liquid contents of the puncheon) by the over-proof strength, and divide the result by 100; the result, added to the ullage, gives the number of proof gallons.

Example To reduce a cask of 97 gallons, 41 per cent over proof, to proof strength:
$$97 \times 41 = 3977$$
$$3977 \div 100 = 39.77$$
$$39.77 + 97 = 136.77 \text{ or number of proof gallons required}$$

The actual contents having been thus ascertained and checked by the result of the Customs re-examination, the Rum is entered on a daily account of receipt for payment.

The quantity of Rum *paid for* is that shown on the 'Landing Account', *ie,* it is the number of gallons contained in the cask when first imported and put into bond.

The quantity *taken on charge,* is that ascertained at the 're-examination' by the Customs authorities, and checked at Deptford, *ie,* the *actual* contents of the casks. The difference between these quantities does not appear in the Yard Accounts at all.

On the Account of Receipt, the quantity to be paid for and the quantity actually received and taken on charge, are shown separately.

The Strong Rum thus received is put into the cellars until required for filling up the vats: the process of starting into the vats is as follows:

The Rum is started into the vats which are all connected one with the other, although any one or more can be shut off, with such a quantity of water as will, it is estimated, reduce it as nearly as possible to issuing strength (4.5 under Proof) but as it would be difficult to hit off this strength precisely in all the 32 vats, two of them, (Nos 1 and 2), containing 17,960 and 17,820 gallons respectively, are appropriated as issuing vats in which the spirit is always kept at the precise issuing strength.

In calculating the quantity of water to be added to a given quantity of strong Rum to reduce it to issuing strength, the following has been the method hitherto adopted.

Multiply the quantity to be reduced by the actual strength, and divide the result by the issuing strength: the difference between this result and the quantity to be reduced gives the number of gallons of water to be added.

Example To reduce 100 gallons at 40 per cent over proof, to issuing strength (4.5 UP) proof spirit being represented by 100.
$$100 \times 140 = 14,000$$
$$14,000 \div 95.5 = 146.59$$
$$146.59 - 100 = 46.59 \text{ or quantity of water to be added in gallons.}$$
The Spirit Reducing Tables recently published by Mr J B Keene, of Her Majesty's Customs, have now, however, enabled a more accurate system to be adopted: briefly stated the rule is as follows:

'Divide the higher of the strengths by the lower to the third decimal, which will give the bulk to which each gallon at the present strength will be raised when reduced as required. Multiply this bulk by the gravity in the Table opposite the required strength, and from the product subtract the gravity for the present strength. The difference multiplied by the present number of gallons will give the quantity of water in gallons: or by moving the decimal points one place to the right, the quantity in pounds.'

The principal causes of loss are evaporation and absorption. As regards the former, the inevitable loss is slightly increased by the fact that the cellars in which the puncheons are stowed before being vatted are not specially well adapted for the purpose, there being too free a current of air, which, however, every effort is made to exclude: the average loss from this cause alone, according to the scale of allowances authorised by the Customs, is as follows:

> For periods not exceeding 1 month   1.5 per cent
> For periods not exceeding 2 months   3 per cent
> For periods not exceeding 6 months   5 per cent

The operations of vatting and drawing off involve a further loss, according to the same authorised scale, of 1 per cent, so that it will be seen that the normal loss, namely 3.74, of Rum from the time it is received at the Yard to the time of issue compares favourably with the percentage of loss which is considered by experts to be fairly attributable to natural causes, and for which therefore, in the case of private firms, allowance is made as a matter of course.

In taking stock, the quantity remaining in the vats is ascertained by the marked gauge glass which is fitted to each vat, and shows the contents in gallons, the quantity being verified by dipping with a gauging rod.

The strength is ascertained by taking samples at various depths by means of a bottle attached to a cord, the samples being tested by Sikes' Hydrometer.

On receipt of an order to send Rum to a Foreign Depôt, or one of the other Home Yards, or of a demand from a Ship, the Rum is drawn off into casks where it remains with the bungs loose for a few days, until a shipping order is received; the casks are then filled up to make good any absorption that has occurred, and the bungs driven in and shived off.

F H Miller Superintendent
Deptford, March 1888

APPENDIX II
Historical note on beer in the Royal Navy

It is impossible to pinpoint that moment when beer first became associated with the navy. By the late 1500's, the service seems to have been largely subsisting on a gallon of beer per day, biscuit and salt meat.

By 1700, there are records of two kinds of beer in issue — a harbour beer (known as Petty Warrant beer), and a stronger Sea beer. The prices then were forty-eight shillings and fifty-six shillings respectively for a tun of two hundred and forty gallons. At this time, beer was obtained mainly from local brewers, but the navy was also operating its own brewhouses at Rotherhithe and Plymouth. Later on, the Admiralty took care to include brewhouses in all three royal victualling yards set up at Deptford, Gosport and Plymouth. In the Royal William Yard at Plymouth, the brewhouse block still stands.

The production and supply figures in the eighteenth century were enormous so it is not surprising that official records reflect the problems and difficulties. There is a fascinating report by a House of Commons Committee appointed in 1710 to enquire into 'Frauds and Abuses' perpetrated in the handling of beer. Among other things, it was alleged that at Rotherhithe, those in charge were taking, 'large quantities of the best and strongest worts for their own use' and then making up by adding water 'so that the sailors and their full proportion of Drink, but the strength and Heart of the beer was left behind in the Brewhouse cellars'.

Abuses were widespread. Brewers under contract obtained fictitious receipts from ships for much more beer than they delivered, sent in their bills to the Admiralty, and then split the proceeds with the ships' pursers. One of the seven gentlemen examined, a Member of Parliament, confessed to making out bills for some two million gallons in the year 1709, having supplied only just over half that amount. Since he had also charged for the non-existent casks, the committee reckoned the year's loss to the Queen at £18,000. The House of Commons expelled the said Mr Thomas Ridge and recommended prosecution. However, fifty years later, a *Sir* Thomas Ridge, probably his son, was still putting in tenders for supplying beer at Portsmouth.

Problems arose over beer's keeping qualities. No dependence could be placed on ale brewed in hot weather, so the process usually began in October and continued throughout the winter. Even then, beer would keep onboard for only a few weeks.

Stowage was another problem. Ships were allowed to take aboard only as much beer as could be conveniently stowed after receiving full supplies of food, sometimes supplemented with wine and spirit which took less room than beer. Occasionally, because of beer shortages, the navy substituted porter; the daily ration was then cut by a half. Porter is referred to in a 1797 pamphlet entitled *The Seaman's Guide showing How to Live Comfortably at Sea* which included a recipe by the German chemist Glauber for concentrating beer. First it had to be boiled to make porter, then was diluted with water and re-fermented. Much effort was expended on solving the problem of concentrating or dehydrating beer on board to save space. The records of 1796 include an instruction to Portsmouth that, 'the whole of the ingredients and apparatus for the purpose of making trial of the efficacy of the plan, invented by Sir John Dalrymple for brewing beer onboard', was to be sent to him at his station in Quiberon Bay.

But nothing came of it, and beer was increasingly superseded by spirit or wine: It was no longer supplied after 1831. Nevertheless, the navy regarded beer highly and the naval brewhouses continued supplying it as a medical comfort for the sick until 1870.

The Admiralty tried to furnish beer aboard ships in World War Two, a matter given considerable impetus by one of those characteristic decisions of Sir Winston Churchill who, in 1943, ordered that beer was to be provided for the armed forces, particularly the large concentrations in the middle and far east.

It so happened that recreation or 'amenity ships' as they were called, were already planned for Pacific Fleet support, and the idea was suggested that brewery plants should be installed aboard, together with malt extract and hop concentrate. This posed many problems — distillation, refrigeration, pasteurisation and so on. The Brewers' Society and many companies were extremely helpful. The Admiralty owed a particular debt to Mr L McMullen of Arthur Guinness, Son and Co, who was serving in the navy at the time, and who was attached to the director of victualling to take charge of the project. When the first ship fitted out in Vancouver, he flew there with a specially selected yeast strain to be used as a 'starter'.

Only one brewery plant in the amenity ship *Menestheus* was put into operation before Japan surrendered. Known to the Navy as 'The Davy Jones brewery — The world's only floating brewery', she produced — needless to say — Davy Jones ale, the technical description of which was 'A chilled carbonated and filtered mild ale of original gravity 1037 deg and colour fifty per cent Lovibond'.

Post war, there were hopes that concentrated beer would help to defeat the chronic shortage of space in modern warships. The Admiralty had kept in touch with the current research in this field by the Brewers' Society and the Brewing Industry Research Foundation. One problem had always been the weight and space of the necessary plant. Luckily, great strides were made with canned beer of which adequate stocks could be carried onboard in NAAFI's charge for the daily issue.

Appendix III
The Cooper and his art

The fellowship of coopers of ancient origin had close links with the City of London. Various ordinances affecting the trade were enforced from as far back as the fourteenth century. Those so employed gained increasing recognition until in 1501, by charter of King Henry VII, the Company was incorporated 'a fraternity or gild for ever'. The charter, described them at that time as 'Citizens and Coopers or the art and mistery of Coopers of the City of London', which was confirmed in 1662 by Charles II.

Few followed the profession but, employed on a piecework principle, each man's output was considerable. They played a vital part in providing storage for the navy's food and drink spanning many centuries, and notably for rum until its abolition in 1970. Prime American white oak was used for the manufacture of rum casks for the reason that it improved the taste and the quality of the spirit if allowed to age. The passing of the navy's rum ration almost signalled the end of the cooper and his particular art, but fortunately it lingers in Scotland where wooden casks benefit the storage of whisky.

The Master Cooper as the name implies, was in charge of production in the victualling yards and the *Book of Cooperage Instructions* issued more than a hundred years ago ordered '. . . that the old staves which may be in his charge are to be worked up into casks, in preference to using new timber, and that he is never to convert new staves into scantling for dry casks when he may have old staves which can possibly be applied thereto'. At the time of the Napoleonic wars, the large fleet in being placed enormous demands on the coopers' output, and to prevent a crisis in the supply of casks, ships were under strict instructions to return staves from 'shaken' casks. Stacks of old staves were preserved in the yards so that when new casks were 'raised' (built), they were made up from the staves of other casks, the process entailing the taking of timber from larger casks or barrels and reducing them for smaller ones. The cooperage employed great frugality and nothing was wasted; even the shavings and sawdust were put to good use in what was known as the 'trusso' ceremony at the end of the long five-year apprenticeship which embryo coopers had to undertake. The 'trussing' initiation caused the apprentice to be placed in the barrel he had made (usually nothing less than a fifty-four gallon hogshead), being pelted with the shavings, sawdust and feathers, and then rolled up and down once for each cooper employed in his workplace.

The manufacturing process which follows is no longer practised in the navy, but is still alive elsewhere. A cooper's success lies in his skill to 'dress' (shape) the staves to obtain the essential uniform thickness, and then joint piece to the correct pitch required according to the varying widths of the timbers. These preparatory operations are carried out entirely by eye, no measurement by rule being used. The staves are 'stood up' by the cooper in preparation for 'firing' and 'trussing'. He employs his own gobbledegook for each stage of the operation and styles this part 'Raising the cask into truss'.

The cask to be, known at this moment as the 'case', is placed over a slow-burning oak-chip fire in an open iron crisset. It is necessary for the fire to be set alight at the top that it may burn down slowly to give the gradual heat necessary for bending the staves. The correct heat can be determined only by touch after long experience, and when it has been attained, the cooper calls out 'Trusso' when, with assistance, he gradually drives down a wooden hoop (known as the 'over-runner' and made of ash), over the pitch — or the widest external dimension of the case. At the top end, what is called the 'pitch hoop' is placed and tightened into position. The case is then reversed, the over-runner re-tightened, and the back-end pitch hoop placed in position.

Once this has been done, the staves are mopped freely with water, thereby softening the timber and making all stave joints liquid tight.

The case now needs a second firing process, fiercer than the first, and termed 'blazing off'. At the correct moment for completing the trussing operation, the case is removed from the fire and 'Trusso' again is called. A final inspection of the finished cask is carried out by the master or senior cooper. By the use of a special lamp which is pushed into the bunghole, he satisfies himself that it is sound in all respects. The 'heads' or lids of the cask are then painted before the finished product begins its active use. If properly looked after, it will last for up to thirty years, with the help of a little first-aid along the way.

The cooper was one of the more highly-paid craftsmen in Admiralty service, and he could make on average, twenty to twenty-five casks per week. At one time the Royal Clarence Yard rolled, or 'poked' as the expression was, two hundred casks or barrels a day, but towards the end a hundred casks each week was the maximum output.

Only after years of experience was the cooper able to make use of the traditional tools of his trade. Only in a cooperage would you be likely to hear of trussing adze, cooper's auger, crozebord, bent shave, and the chive and iron, all of which should find their places in museums to make up for their loss of an active role.

APPENDIX IV
Dutch and French navies

The Netherlands The crews of Dutch warships were supplied with water and beer during the first half of the seventeenth century. During the Second English War, 1665-1667 (the Second Dutch War to British historians), mention is made of the use of brandy by both officers and seamen but seamen were undoubtedly given a daily ration of beer. Not until 1692 was jenever (Dutch gin) drunk onboard warships. Beer remained the normal drink for sailors as in the British navy, but increasingly 'maltbrandy' or jenever were supplied. Onboard the *Overijssel* bills show that beer to the value of f774,00 was bought, and jenever to the value of only f12,00. During the eighteenth century jenever came more into its own as a precaution against disease, especially on long journeys. The ration then was fifty grams a day. It is interesting to note that the Dutch word for a ration of gin (dram), *oorlam*, also meant 'an old and experienced seaman' according to nautical dictionaries. Hence it is quite possible that *oorlam* was used to define the gin ration because it was supplied only to the older sailors.

In 1899, Parliament decided that the jenever ration should be restricted to sailors more than twenty years old, and then only if requested by them. Younger men were given the option of coffee or cocoa. The Minister for the Navy, himself a naval officer, did not consider that the jenever ration would lead to abuse; he rated it a healthy drink in cold and heavy weather. However, coffee was already being issued during the night watches instead of an extra issue of jenever.

During the voyage of *HNLMS Zeeland* from Den Helder to Curacao in early March 1899, five cents a day was paid experimentally to those who did not want their fifty-gram jenever ration and some twenty per cent of the crew opted for cash. Then it was discovered that five cents would buy twice the daily jenever ration ashore resulting in five men who did not even draw the ration being punished for drunkenness!

Finally, the jenever ration was abolished by royal decree of February 14, 1905, except that it could still be issued for medical reasons. After 1905, men were allowed a daily ration of two bottles of beer per person. In wardrooms, gunrooms and petty officers' messes, there was greater choice of alcoholic drinks. Since July 1, 1979, the consumption of alcohol has been prohibited during normal working hours, including lunchtime, aboard ship and in naval barracks.

France The essential alcoholic difference between the French and British navies is that whereas the British started with beer and changed to rum, wine has been constantly preferred by the French. It has fulfilled a double role in the French navy in that its consumption has not only been a concession to national habits, but has also served as compensation for the rigours of life at sea. Records show that wine — usually claret — was supplied in the seventeenth century at a daily rate of three-quarters of a litre, a privilege that has continued, with varying quantities, until today. It is served with the main meals. The French navy is still 'wet'.

The problems faced by French and British alike in providing alcoholic refreshment for ships' companies are strikingly similar. Wine, as with beer, was supplied in cask. Usually immature, it went sour fairly quickly. For this reason, and space limitations, French ships destined for foreign service could stow only limited quantities in their holds.

When the wine had been drunk after several weeks at sea, eau-de-vie was issued as a substitute at three-sixteenths of a litre per day (a quarter of the normal wine ration). Brandy needed less stowage but, equally, was less beneficial to health. Colbert, Louis XIV's brilliant Minister of Marine, limited its use to tropical waters. Wine, of course, possessed anti-scorbutic qualities which gave it another advantage over eau-de-vie.

Cider and beer were also available to the French navy from time to time through the eighteenth century and when used as substitutes for wine, double quantities were issued. Because of the extra space needed for their stowage, they were never popular (at least to the administrators!). They were supplied usually only when ships were employed for short spells at sea in the colder climates.

Under their method of enlistment, French crews were often made up of men from the same region, sharing similar habits and customs. Thus, depending on whether they were Bretons or Provencaux for example, they would possess certain characteristics. Bretons, recruited largely from fishermen, were noted for their indulgence — if not over-indulgence — in alcohol. They liked to hoard their ration during the week to become fighting drunk on Sunday (Saturday night for the British sailor). Apparently it was looked upon with benevolence and understanding by French officers, unlike the British Navy where it constituted a serious offence.

Did the French ever drink rum? Well yes, if rarely. Records show that tafia (rum distilled from molasses), was occasionally issued, but never became paramount as in the British navy.

APPENDIX V
Short glossary

Buffer The chief bos'n's mate; the 'buffer' or go between

Bulling or 'bull the cask' To make grog by the simple — and not always successful — method of pouring water into an empty rum cask and letting it stand and soak

Bung up and bilge free Technically the proper stowage for a rum cask, but also used to describe anyone lying asleep during a 'make and mend'

Crusher Regulating petty officer or ship's policeman

Dead Marine An empty bottle that has done its duty and is ready to do it again

Dram Old term for a neat rum ration

Fanny Rum receptacle for ships' messes. Full origin already given in text page 150

Firkin Ten gallon cask

Flip A sailor's drink in harbour of beer fortified with rum or brandy which had been smuggled onboard

Gulpers Gift of extra grog for a big favour. Usually about one third of the tot

Hogshead Fifty-four-fifty-six gallon cask

Jack Nastyface Name by which the cook's assistant was known

Jack Dusty Rating of the victualling branch responsible for the book-keeping of the daily rum issue

Jaunty The master-at-arms. Possibly a corruption of the French 'gendarme'

Jimmy Bungs The cooper — usually relating to the cooper onboard ship when carried

Kilderkin Eighteen gallon cask

Killick Ancient anchor but also the name given to a leading seaman or leading hand

Nelson's blood The name given to rum after Trafalgar in the erroneous belief that Lord Nelson's body was conveyed back to England preserved in a barrel of neat rum. In fact, brandy and spirit of wine were used.

Pipes or Tommy Pipes The boatswain

Plushers The residue of grog in a ship's mess after each man has had his ration

Puncheon Cask holding about a hundred gallons

Quarter cask Half a hogshead or twenty-seven to twenty-eight gallons

Queen's A method employed for obtaining extra rum at the expense usually of messmates by inserting a thumb in the measure when pouring

Rumbullion, Rumbustion, Kill Devil, Barbados Waters, Red-eye, Saccharum, Nelson's Blood Alternative names for rum, all of ancient origin

Rum bos'n (bubbly bos'n) The member of a mess collecting its daily grog

Rum rat One possessing a 'good nose' for extra rum

Sandy bottoms Very rare gift of a whole tot for an enormous favour

Scuttled butt Water butt used on deck with hole in top or removable lid for dipping purposes

Shake the cask To knock the hoops off and lash the staves together in a bundle. All loose staves were called shakes when a cask was broken up

Sippers Gift of extra grog for a small favour. Usually about one-fifth of a tot

Spruce beer A beer made by adding young fir cones to fermented malt. A good antidote to scurvy

Sucking the monkey Unlawful way of obtaining liquor by employing means such as substituting the milk of a coconut

Tanky Originally the Navigator's or Master's assistant responsibe for the fresh water tanks of the ship. Man detailed or selected to help with the daily rum issue in more recent times

'Tea chest' The nickname given to *HMS Thetis* in which the experiment was carred out in 1823 of halving the rum ration and issuing tea and sugar in lieu

Ullage The residue of grog at the major issuing ceremony to rum bos'ns

BIBLIOGRAPHY

Ballard, Admiral G A *The black battlefleet*
Baynham, H *Before the mast*
Beaglehole, J C *The edited journals of Captain James Cook (3 vols)*
Churchill, W S *A history of the English speaking peoples (4 vols)*
Clowes, W Laird *The Royal Navy (7 vols)*
Coulter and Lloyd *Medicine and the Navy*
Drake, Francis *The world encompassed 1577 - 80*
Dugan, J *The great mutiny*
Dundas, Admiral Sir C *An Admiral's yarn*
Ford, D *Admiral Vernon and the Navy*
Granville, W *Sea slang*
Hampshire, A C *Just an old naval custom*
Hough, R *Captain Bligh and Mr Christian*

Kemp, P *The British sailor*
Lewis, M A *The Navy of Britain, a Social History of the Royal Navy 1793 - 1815*
    The Navy in transition
    England's sea officers
Lloyd, C *The British Seaman*
    St Vincent and Camperdown
Lowis, G L *Fabulous Admirals*
Lowry *The origins of some naval terms and customs*
Marcus, G J *The age of Nelson*
Masefield, J *Sea life in Nelson's time*
Neale, W J *Gentleman Jack*
Oman, C *Nelson*
Parkinson, C Northcote *Portsmouth Point*
Rasor, B L *Reform in the Royal Navy*
Warner, O *The British Navy*
Winton, J *Hurrah for the life of a sailor*

Other publications consulted

Admiralty Circulars
Brassey's Naval Annual
Manual of Seamanship
Naval and Military Record
Naval Court Martial Returns
Navy Records Society *The Vernon Papers, Naval Administration 1715 - 50, The Royal Navy and North America, The Health of Seamen, The Keith Papers, The Sandwich Papers.*
Queen's (or King's) Regulations and Admiralty Instructions
Rum — store, accounting and operating instructions (BR 95)
The Mariner's Mirror Vols 1, 6 and 41
The Nautical Magazine
The Naval Chronicle (1799 - 1815)
The Naval Review
The Regulations and Instructions relating to His Majesty's service at sea
The Victualling Manual (BR 93)
United States naval institute proceedings

Index